VALUING THE FUTURE

A conversation about investment

BEN PATON

First published in 2012 by
Sociables Publishing

PUBLISHER'S NOTE

A CIP Catalogue of this book is available from
the British Library

ISBN: 978-0-9570396-1-2

Diagrams by Ben Paton
Cover illustration and cartoons by Chris Duggan

'When one looks back it has always been the case that
investment and civilisation have walked a tightrope. They have
always seemed at risk of falling off the rope into an abyss of
chaos and disintegration.'

CHANDLER®
BOOK DESIGN

Typeset in Sabon 10pt by
www.chandlerbookdesign.co.uk

Printed and distributed by
Lightning Source Inc.

VALUING THE FUTURE

A conversation about investment

BEN PATON

Published by Sociables Publishing

www.valuingthefuture.com

CONTENTS

VALUING THE FUTURE

For Andrea, Julia and Arthur

Preface

> '*In this age of specialization men who thoroughly know one field are often incompetent to discuss another. The great problems of the relations between one and another aspect of human activity have for this reason been discussed less and less in public. ... The old problems, such as the relation of science and religion, are still with us, and I believe present as difficult dilemmas as ever, but they are not often publicly discussed because of the limitations of specialization.*'
>
> – Richard Feynman, *American physicist*

This book is structured as a conversation between a young man looking to invest and an eccentric 'financial adviser'. The financial adviser does not have any products to sell, only opinions on what investment is about and how to do it successfully.

Although there's a logical thread to the discussion, the conversation ranges widely across many subject areas not commonly included in 'how to get rich quick' books about investment. The real world is surreal and paradoxical and opposites can co-exist and be simultaneously 'true'. The discussion throws up some of these paradoxes and shows that substance may differ from form. The aim of the book is to stimulate interest in investment and finance in general.

This book tries to explain why individuals and societies invest, what it means to invest and how investment works. Its aim is to promote understanding without prescribing what anyone might do with their knowledge. No stocks are peddled and no particular strategies are promoted.

Who this book is for

> *'The ability to express an idea is well nigh as important as the idea itself.'*
> – Bernard Baruch

> *'Everything you do is based on a theory.'*
> – Anon

This book is for anyone curious about business, finance and investment. It answers some apparently simple questions such as:

- How do investors get out more than they put in?
- What role does time play in investment?
- What is capital and why should it be rewarded?
- What is an asset?
- What is economic value and how does it differ from other notions of value and worth?
- What are money and credit and how are they created?
- What are returns and how can they be measured?
- What are interest rates? What do they price?
- Why do some businesses make high returns and some low returns?
- What is a business model?
- How are businesses valued?
- What is risk?

The answers are based on a mixture of theory and my practical experience as an equity fund manager. I have tried to offer the sort of 'avuncular' advice on how finance and business works that I should have liked to have received as a teenager when thinking about what sort of career to go into. What sort of advice would I have wanted an uncle to give? If I had been capable of expressing it, I would have wanted to have a holistic or 'system level' explanation, which is another way of saying a view of how the different parts of 'the system' integrate.

Some explanations are akin to journalism. They explain 'big events' by describing the key players and their motives. Major takeovers, bank failures and economic crises make the news. *Barbarians at the Gate* (HarperCollins, 1990) is a great account of the leveraged buyout of RJR Nabisco, for example. But decades later the detail is of less interest, the players are forgotten and the events prove ephemeral.

A useful explanation stands the test of time because it describes a continuing framework that remains the same or similar, even as the people come and go. Details date quickly. Abstractions from the detail are theories, but have more chance of being of continuing interest. An explanation that stands the test of time offers a description of how the system works, rather than what its particular outcomes were at particular times.

The whole is more than the sum of the parts

*'We are in an age that assumes the narrowing trends
of specialization to be logical, natural, and desirable.
Consequently, society expects all earnestly responsible
communication to be crisply brief. … In the meantime,
humanity has been deprived of comprehensive understanding. Specialization has bred feelings of isolation,
futility, and confusion in individuals. It has also resulted in the individual's leaving responsibility for thinking
and social action to others. Specialization breeds biases
that ultimately aggregate as international and ideologi-
cal discord, which, in turn, leads to war.'*

– Buckminster Fuller, *architect and futurist*

I was inspired by Ernst Gombrich who wrote a book called *A
Short History of the World for Young Readers*[1] – which narrates
the history of the world from the 'beginning of time'. In his
Little History Gombrich tried to integrate different subjects to
give an 'all-round' view, to try to show how the whole jigsaw
puzzle of human history fits together. Gombrich provides a *tour
d'horizon* and threads a story through it. His book is satisfying
because it is a personal selection and synthesis of what was
important to him. An interpretation of the history of the world
as so much 'sound and fury signifying nothing' might be, from
one perspective, objective if nihilistic. Gombrich, however, puts
his own meaning onto events and it becomes less important
whether the events have objective meaning than that Gombrich's
subjective interpretation is useful and entertaining.

Gombrich's target audience was children, but he is probably
mainly read by adults. Children often ask different questions
from adults. Their questions are more searching because they

---

[1] First published in 1936 and translated into English in 2005 as
    A Little History of the World.

are more naive. 'Why is the sky blue?' is a childlike question. Answers can be given on multiple different levels. Answers could involve a discussion of the colour of light, of types of energy, of the sun and the solar system. 'Why' questions are open-ended. They grope for a reason outside a system. If a sequence of 'why' questions is pursued long enough, the answers end in something like 'it just is', or 'nobody knows'.

'How' questions can be answered more satisfactorily. To be able to explain how something works, it is necessary to understand the system of which it is part. The smaller the system, the easier it is to grasp how it works. To explain how the light switch in a kitchen works is quite easy. To explain how the electricity is generated that works the light is more complex. To explain how the political, legal, engineering, accounting and economic systems interact to enable the light switch to work is more complex still. To explain how electrons work is to confront mystery. If it is possible to explain how something works, it is easier to feel and take some responsibility for it.

The book tries to go into enough 'why' questions to give the reader context, and enough 'how' questions to provide some practical explanations.

A tour of the investment horizon

Just as Gombrich gives a tour of the history of the world, the idea for this book was to give a tour of the investment horizon. To describe a complex and dynamic system of systems simply and briefly is not easy. At one level it may be impossible. A description that applies in one jurisdiction may not apply in another; a description of how a system worked in the past may not describe the present or future workings.

One way of addressing the difficulty is to take lots of photographs from many different angles. One picture can be misleading – like the picture of the hotel in the tour operator's brochure that carefully excludes the building site next door. A combination of several wide-angle shots putting the object into context, and some telephoto shots of particular details can give a useful overall impression.

Wide-angle views put things in context – they literally show the background, the lie of the land. Wide-angle shots of investment include some view of time, of accounting assets and liabilities, of law and politics, of economics and the natural environment, of the money and credit system, and of currencies.

Telephoto views of investment need to focus on the details of how specific generic business models make money, how economic value is measured, and how profits and returns are calculated.

Taking the photo collection together one can form a gestalt – a view of how the whole fits together. To get the right perspective on risk, price and valuation, one has to keep an eye on the foreground and the background, the subject as well as the object.

The book tries to be accessible enough not to bore a curious layman with too many technicalities. It tries to distinguish between those elements of investment that are objective – where objective arithmetic can be performed – and those parts that are subjective, to give readers sufficient notion of the complications to allow them to apply the technicalities in a practical way.

I hope I have offered a sympathetic description of the way markets work – particularly equity markets. Modern economies, trade, banking and technologies and their interaction are complicated. On occasion and in some important respects they do not always work. It is a very imperfect world but it is also a paradoxical world, simultaneously perfect and imperfect, in which attempts to make matters more perfect often end up making them more imperfect. Markets are often criticised by people who have little sympathy for them, who would prefer to substitute dogmatic opinion and interference for Adam Smith's 'invisible hand'. Such people remind me of the expression, 'Don't let the perfect solution get in the way of a good solution.' For all their failings, market-oriented systems deliver the standard of living that we enjoy in Europe and North America. Our standard of living depends on market systems. So it is important to understand them well enough to fine tune them, rather than end up throwing spanners into the works.

Acknowledgements

The seeds of many of the ideas in this book have been planted over many years by too many people to mention. I owe a debt of gratitude to the many talented 'sell side' and 'buy side' analysts I have worked with in the City. I am particularly grateful to Michael Howell and Hari Krishnan of CrossBorder Capital and to Edgar Allen, Mark Ayling, Ed Moran, Marcus Edwards-Jones, Richard Colvile, Simon de Borchgrave, Emma Duckworth and Martina Keens-Betts for reading a draft and offering valuable comments.

'When a thing is intelligible you have a sense of participation. When a thing is unintelligible you have a sense of estrangement. ... If the mind cannot bring to the world a set, or, shall we say, a tool box, of powerful ideas the world must appear to it as a chaos, a mass of unrelated phenomena, of meaningless events. Such a man is like a person in a strange land without any signs of civilization, without maps, or signposts or indicators of any kind.'

E.F. Schumacher, *economist and advocate of 'intermediate' technologies*

'... we leave behind us the world of historical iron-masters and banker-historians, geological divines and scholar tobacconists, with its genial watchword: to know something of everything and everything of something and through the gateway of Competitive Examination we enter into the Wasteland of Experts, each knowing so much about so little that he can neither be contradicted nor is worth contradicting.'

G.M. Young, *Victorian England, Portrait of an Age*

CHAPTER 1

Should I invest?

'To trace something unknown back to something known is alleviating, soothing, gratifying and gives moreover a feeling of power. Danger, disquiet, anxiety attend the unknown – the first instinct is to eliminate these distressing states. First principle: any explanation is better than none... The cause-creating drive is thus conditioned and excited by the feeling of fear...'

– Friedrich Nietzsche, *German philosopher*

A man takes Friday afternoon off work and goes to see an adviser – a money adviser. He has some questions.

Should I invest? *he asks.*

Well, *says the adviser*, you are already investing all the time.

What do you mean?

Every time you create a stock of stuff that you do not consume today, you are investing.

What do you mean, 'a stock of stuff'?

Some things you do and buy are consumed immediately. The meal you buy at the restaurant today has no re-sale value tomorrow. Today's meal will not exist tomorrow. You can't eat the same meal twice. Meals are stuff that flows quickly.

Some things you buy today you can consume tomorrow or next year or in a decade's time. If you buy a house and live in it, you will be able to 'consume' it next year and every year until you sell it. If you buy a car today, you can consume it tomorrow and the day after. The rate at which you consume your car depends on how many miles you drive, how well you maintain it and what sort of resale value it may have if you ever wish to sell it.

Everything flows, but some stuff flows more slowly. It collects in eddies and pools in the stream and forms reservoirs that can be called on later. Stuff that does not flow fast, that is not consumed immediately, and that can be called on later is an investment for the future.

Aren't you supposed to ask me about my attitude to risk and then help me weigh up bonds versus equities?

I don't think your attitude to risk is the right question. Risk is about consequences. Some consequences can be estimated with mathematical precision and some elude quantification even after the event – because the alternative histories that might have followed from different choices are unknown and possibly unknowable.

You see risk means different things to different people. A few people might talk about risk in terms of 'mean variance' analysis. Others may be guessing consequences based on experience or gut feel. Most people don't have an off pat definition of risk and most don't think about their attitude to it very often.

The question is based on the premise that if you want high returns, you must take high risk. If you say you want low risk, you may be recommended to stay in cash or buy a government bond – which exposes you to interest rate risk if you sell before maturity, and inflation risk if you don't sell before maturity. If you say you want high returns then you may be recommended to go into equities, which will give you risk but not necessarily high returns. The trouble is that the variability of stockmarket prices is not a complete description of risk, and the relationship between risk and return is not straightforward. Indeed, it is often paradoxical; apparently risky situations may be fully discounted in the price and apparently safe situations (like bonds) may fail to discount the risks. There is only one intelligent answer to the question 'Do you want to take risks?': you want to take risks which you believe are attractively priced in relation to your view of the consequences and your balance sheet.

Okay – then what matters?

I would suggest that your attitude to the future matters. It matters more than your attitude to risk.

So why does my attitude to the future matter?

Because the future is where the consequences happen. If you did not care at all about the future, your anxiety would not have risen to a level high enough to drive you to come and see me in the first place. So you must be concerned. What you really, really want is an insurance policy for future consequences, to 'future proof' yourself.

Without some view of the future it is difficult or impossible to have a view on value. And without some view on value it is difficult or impossible to know what risk you may be taking.

I'm not at all sure I agree with that.

The trouble with getting into a discussion about any subject with which everyone has some acquaintance is that everyone is working off presuppositions without necessarily putting the presuppositions onto the table and examining them.

Although we start out assuming we are talking about the same thing it can transpire, after a while, that we have been each talking about different things! In other words, that we have been at cross purposes.

So what are the presuppositions we should get on the table?

You are right. We need to spend a moment to talk about what we are going to talk about, to set an agenda if you like.

You have asked me an unusual question, *should* I invest? Most people come in having already decided to invest and ask the question *what* should I invest in? *Should* questions are implicitly judgmental. They have a moral angle.

You have also immediately asked about risk. Risk is a small word with big implications. To go straight to risk is to start at the end of the analysis rather than at the beginning. It is often a good idea to jump to the conclusion and then work back. But risk is about trade-offs and comparisons of possible outcomes. It is difficult to think about the probabilities before first considering the possibilities. It can be difficult to imagine all the consequences. Experience can broaden what people imagine is possible and refine their view of what is probable.

So what should we put on the agenda?

We ought to define what we mean by investment.

We ought to define the investment 'universe'. What *sorts* of things can we invest in?

We could then discuss the differences between investing cash and investing time.

Once we've narrowed the problem down to investing cash we need consider what we mean by an asset. When we have defined assets we can decide which subset of assets serve different purposes and which are more attractive.

So how do you define investment?

Investment is a very terrestrial, temporal activity. It is about accumulating or maintaining capabilities in the present in order to provide some flow of resources or services in the future.

Time pervades everything to do with investment. Capital and income are defined by time. Capital is a stock at a moment of time and income is a flow per unit of time. Individuals accumulate savings, which they hope will generate an income later. Societies accumulate real and financial capital in order to deliver a flow of resources as and when they are needed.

What do people invest?

The apparently obvious answer is money. But money is only a symbol for resources and a rather imperfect symbol.

Not everyone has money. But everyone has time which they are consciously or unconsciously investing. Time, and how people 'spend' their time, is closely associated with the difficult notion of 'value'.

And how do you define the investment 'universe'?

The investment universe is what people spend their time and money on.

The investment universe is very broad.

People invest their time into several generic sorts of things and the implicit 'rules of the game' are different in each case.

At one end of the spectrum time is invested in activities without an expectation of any monetary reward or compensation.

'Not-for-money' activities make up a huge part of people's lives. For some sorts of societies not-for-money activity is the only activity. In a 'Western' economy the not-for-money economy is still very large: it is the world of families and hobbies and gift exchange.

At the other end of the spectrum there are 'for-money' activities. The most important of these in a developed economy is usually working for money or monetary compensation.

Both 'for money' and 'not-for-money' activities take place in organisations. A family is an organisation, though few families consciously think of themselves as such. So is a school or a civil service or an army or a business.

In some 'not-for-money' organisations money is not even the medium of exchange. The functions which family members perform are seldom remunerated with money. In other 'not-for-money' organisations the members of the organisation are paid in money but the value of the service they supply is difficult to measure in money terms. So for example an army supplies defence services for which there is typically no market and no market price. Citizens are implicitly paying for 'defence services' as part of their taxes. But the money cost to the 'consumer' of the defence service is not explicit and would be difficult to work out.

That's an unusually broad definition of the investment universe!

Yes. Books about investment often define the universe much more narrowly. Not-for-money activities are not considered to be investments. But of course the whole of Nature is a not-for-money activity! Natural and social phenomena which are not 'priced' are outside conventional investment.

Money is to our civilisation what water is to fish. It is so pervasive it is taken for granted. So it is easy to forget that money is not the only medium of exchange, that money is not itself 'value' but only a token of some other value. People do not always devote a lot of time to considering what their underlying values are.

Looking at a broader definition helps to remind us that investment as conventionally defined is a rather narrow activity. It concerns itself with an even narrower subset of 'for-money' activities. Within for-money activity, most professional investment confines itself to investment in financial assets.

I'm more familiar with the expressions 'for profit' and 'not for profit'

It is not so common in developed economies to distinguish between for-money and not-for-money activities. One reason is that what gets managed is what has been measured. No one fills in time sheets to account for how they spend their not-for-money time. Money is much easier to measure than time. If something is not measured, it is difficult to talk about, and to that extent it does not 'exist'.

Some organisations describe themselves as 'not for profit'. The distinction between for profit and not-for-profit organisations is not necessarily very great. They both aim to make cash surpluses. The main difference is that the surpluses or 'profits' of a not-for-profit organisation do not belong to shareholders.

For-money and not-for-money activities seem to belong to different universes.

It is as if they are in two 'parallel' universes which operate according to rather different rules.

Families are in a universe where gifts are the currency that circulates and makes the world go around. In this universe, life is itself a gift, health is a gift, children are gifts, education is a gift and talents are gifts. You cannot usually literally buy these gifts in a market. You can't pay the bees to pollinate your apple tree or the blackbirds to nest in your garden for you to show your children or the butterflies to visit your flowers for you to admire – although a garden centre will try to sell you something to help. They just arrive until, like the sparrows of my childhood, they disappear. Life cannot be purchased – at least in most places most of the time. Most people accept that it has an element of the unfathomable mystery, if not the divine, and is outside market economics. In the earliest civilisations, this universe was probably the main universe and economics was subsumed within it. So people did not make 'investments' so much as make gifts that bore offspring. Seeds and animals were given and multiplied themselves and gifts were given to the gods to facilitate the cycle. Market economics was something that was done with foreigners and strangers; if done with friends and family it was 'usury' and frowned on or prohibited.

The market versus the 'gift economy'

So what is the market universe?

The other universe is the market, which is governed by exchange relationships. The essence of a market exchange is that the two parties to the exchange both think they are getting a reasonable deal and once the transaction is settled there is no further obligation on either side.

Perhaps the first person to extol the virtues of the market was Adam Smith, who wrote,

> *'It is not from the benevolence of the butcher, the brewer, or the baker that we expect our dinner, but from their regard for their own interest. We address ourselves not to their humanity but to their self-love and never talk to them of our own necessities but of their own advantages.'*[2]

---

[2] Adam Smith, *The Wealth of Nations*, 1776.

The market is a universe of debtors and creditors – where people create liabilities and settle them and where the settlement extinguishes any obligation. Why do the parties think they are getting a fair deal? Mainly because people accept that the price set by market forces is, generally speaking, a 'fair' price. It also helps that the system is sufficiently transparent that the fairness could in principle be re-examined after the event. The biggest element in 'market forces' is competition. Competition means that the buyer and the seller each have choice, and so the price at which most of the volume is transacted is a market clearing price. Competition is not perfect but it is better than most other systems, and so governments set up watchdogs and regulators to oversee the workings of the market to try to ensure that competition works. Market systems work because most people believe in the intrinsic fairness of the prices which are created.

In the market economy money is the symbol of value. If you do work, you get money in exchange. When you buy something, you get something in exchange for money. If you have none to exchange, by and large you don't get anything. No money in your pocket means nothing to buy in the supermarket. Supermarkets don't do charity, an old-fashioned word for love, or loyalty, or, for the most part, credit. Our relationship with the supermarket – which in reality is a multi-billion transaction/dollar/euro/pound organisation – is a pure exchange relationship. Of course, the marketing people use all the tools available to try to hypnotise us into believing that this relationship can be something more than an exchange relationship. So they come up with 'loyalty cards' and loyalty bonuses. But people are not really fooled by the use of the word 'loyalty'. They know that if they are hard up, there is no point going to the supermarket. They go instead to the 'gift universe' – the world of family and friends and charities, and even departments of government, which are set up to compensate for or provide for the areas of life where the market with its money exchange relationships is inadequate.

This all sounds rather paradoxical.

That's because it is. In the market economy, financial liabilities are created but there are no ongoing social obligations. In families, there are no financial liabilities but there are social obligations. In a market economy, nothing is for free but there is freedom. In families and tribes, many things are 'free' or are given but they come with a commitment to reciprocate, which in many cases constricts freedom. The market does not oblige you to use the same supermarket, restaurant or hotel. You are free to choose. The gift universe does impose an obligation to look after your children and parents and friends in both a financial and social sense. The State recognises these obligations. So in the UK, fathers can be forced to provide for their children. In France, for example, children have a legal right to inherit property from parents: a French child cannot be disinherited. These are examples of how the gift economy constrains freedom in the exchange economy.

The position of women in the economy illustrates how the exchange economy has increased in scope. Not many generations ago in Europe, women were more often than not in the gift economy rather than in the exchange economy. So, for example, at one time most married women did not work in the exchange economy. Instead they worked in the not-for-money, gift economy – they created families, brought up children, did unpaid or charitable work. Over time, as the requirements of war required (WW1 and WW2), as labour-saving devices in the home permitted (electrification) and as mental models of the world changed (voting rights, women's liberation), women moved into the exchange economy – so that now most women in Europe work in the exchange economy. Not many generations ago, women in Europe did not have the right to own property, to vote or to enter certain professions, and some could not marry without a dowry. The exchange economy has brought freedoms for women that they did not previously have. Yet for some people the old 'gift universe' relationships of husbands and wives is still perceived as in some respects an ideal. And in a traditional marriage service daughters are still 'given away' by their fathers.

It seems rather hard to keep these parallel universes separate!

That's because it is. People, most people, are happy with an exchange relationship, which allows them to buy a pound of butter in a supermarket. They are less happy when they are themselves the object of an exchange relationship – as when they are made redundant after many years of 'faithful service'. In the West, most people would now feel outrage at the idea that a human being could be bought and sold as the property of another human being – and yet this was a foundation of Greek and Roman civilisations, and was only abolished in Russia in 1861 and in the United States in 1865. If you were not a citizen, you did not have access to the market to sell your services. Whatever the imperfections of the market universe, at the very least it allows people who do not necessarily share the same view of the world to trade with each other on more or less equal terms.

Some aspects of life fit uncomfortably in a market exchange relationship. Take an army. The glue that holds an army together is based on emotion – camaraderie, loyalty, courage, love of country, devotion to duty. When soldiers die in war most people would be disgusted by the notion that they were adequately paid to do it. They give their lives to a greater cause.

Much of the time people take exchange relationships at face value. Yet further back up the supply chain, there may be much that from a gift relationship perspective they would be very uncomfortable with. One such area is the treatment of animals. The filet of chicken or beef or tuna is one thing when wrapped in cellophane. The living creature that was its source is another. Organisations that depend on gifts – churches, charities like Friends of the Earth or Greenpeace – try to draw attention to some of the areas which the market does not address. The two universes cannot escape from one another. Hardhearted businessmen often give fortunes away to charity. And charities, such as churches, are often some the largest owners of property and hence some of the largest investors in the exchange economy.

These two universes seem to be 'at daggers drawn' with each other.

You are quite right that there is a great deal of mutual distrust, which sometimes descends into hatred, between people who tend to operate mainly in one universe or the other. People who work predominantly in market exchange – such as bond traders – are caricatured as greedy and unscrupulous. People who work in areas where gift exchange predominates – such as academia, or schools – are sometimes caricatured as living in 'ivory towers' and being impractical or sentimental. Society needs both universes – the efficiency of market exchange and the sentiment of gift exchange. Paradoxically both sides subconsciously recognise this and try to 'steal each other's clothes' in their marketing. So businesses claim to be 'caring' and 'passionate' about their products and customers and charities use business measures to demonstrate effectiveness.

Can these universes be reconciled?

They can be reconciled if there is mutual understanding and each acknowledges the right of the other to exist – in fact the complete mutual inter-dependence of the two worlds.

Neither universe can get along without the other. At one extreme there are those who believe that the market is the solution to everything, 'market fundamentalists', as George Soros calls them. At the other extreme are those who believe in collective solutions.

In Europe most countries are organised as mixed, pluralistic 'market democracies'. Some of the factors that reconcile the two perceptions of life are regulation taxation and democratic party politics.

Regulation, taxation and democratic party politics

How do they do that?

Regulation constrains rights of ownership in the public or collective interest. A landowner may own a river, but he may not discharge anything he likes into it or extract unlimited amounts of water. A car manufacturer may own a product, but it must conform with minimum safety standards. An electricity company may own a distribution network but it must allow access to all serious suppliers on fair terms.

Taxation takes money from the market economy and spends it on the gift economy in areas such as health and education. The hard efficiencies of the market economy are accepted because they help pay for the necessities of life which people feel ought to be freely available or free.

Democratic party politics allow people to own or to feel a sense of ownership towards the 'system', the capital stock of the country. There is collective ownership of government assets and democracy gives people a choice of policies and therefore some sense of responsibility towards collective assets. Paradoxically some of the worst management of assets takes place when no one feels a sense of ownership towards the asset. Lack of ownership tends to be accompanied by a sense of powerlessness. The United Nations has presided over military fiascos and corruption in part because responsibility was diluted to the extent that no one felt or took ownership.

Democratic party politics tend to swing like a pendulum between policies that favour market efficiency and policies that favour concepts of social justice. Often particular political parties are more identified with one set of policies than another. This mutual understanding and acceptance has taken centuries to achieve. The market economy grew up in the 16th century as the Protestant Reformation took hold and spread with the Industrial Revolution in the UK and Holland. It has taken multiple revolutions (1830, 1848 and 1870 in Europe, for example) and two world wars for the 'system' to be refined.

In emerging markets the mutual understanding sometimes does not exist. Leaders in some African countries have inherited a legacy of a local tribal 'gift economy' culture, which is thought of as the natural and national culture and elements of an exchange economy, which is in turn thought of as colonial and foreign, even imperialist. Some African leaders have perceived themselves as the 'fathers' of their people, rather than as the chief executives of a government infrastructure created to deliver efficient services. Mutual antipathy between these 'parallel universes' in some African countries has resulted in a collapse of the market economy and huge concomitant inefficiency and corruption. Martin Meredith's history of Africa since 1945, *The State of Africa*, is a brilliant account of what happened.

Investment as implicitly building the future

This is all interesting, if a bit metaphysical, but what has it to do with investment?

More than you might imagine. Investment is all about getting a return. The return you get is conditioned by what you expect to get and by what society will let you get.

What do you mean?

Simply that it helps to know what you are buying into. When you give your time to organise the church fête you expect to take pleasure in the fête and in the pleasure that other people take. You don't expect a financial return. You get a 'psychic income', not a monetary return. When you deposit your money in a bank there's an advertised interest rate and you expect to get your capital back with interest. When you invest in a business you are buying into a part of the exchange economy.

That sounds obvious from a middle-class European or North American perspective. It may not be so obvious if you are in an emerging market or have been living in a Communist regime. You have bought into a system of property rights, regulation, taxation and government. It is a system that affords amazing freedoms, that allows you to invest on the other side of the world in businesses you may never have visited, run by people you have never met.

Is that a good thing?

It is certainly an amazing thing. It brings together 'necessities' of civilisation from all the corners of the world; it brings coal from Russia, South Africa, Indonesia and Australia to generate your electricity; oil from Saudi Arabia to provide transport fuel for your car and heating oil for your home and raw materials for plastics; it brings silicon chips from Taiwan to run electronic devices like computers and mobile phones. The list of interdependencies is endless. It requires international collaboration between businesses, which is often greater than inter-governmental cooperation. There are many imperfect or 'bad' things about it but, whatever one thinks about it, it is what makes and sustains a large part of people's experience of the modern world. Everyone complains about some aspect of it. The price of oil goes up or the price of electricity goes up and politicians complain. Higher prices are, of course, a shock but not as big a shock as discovering that there is no petrol at the petrol station and no electricity for days on end when you flip the light switch. Blackouts are rare in Europe and North America – but they are very common in many emerging markets.

But do I want to invest in it?

In one sense you do not have any choice in the matter. You are already complicit in the exchange economy by being part of it. Short of becoming a hermit, you cannot opt out. And places where you can live as a hermit are already quite crowded! Your taxes are paid to a government that is complicit in all of it and orchestrates large parts of it. If you buy a newspaper, loaf of bread, a computer, a washing machine then your money feeds a supply chain whose roots stretch out to sources of components and raw materials that are global. Even if you make no direct investments yourself, the likelihood is that other people will be making investments on your behalf. If you pay taxes to the government, it is investing on your behalf. If you contribute to a pension plan, someone is investing on your behalf, and if you leave your money in the bank, someone is investing the money to enable the bank to pay interest on your deposit. There's no getting away from it. Opt-out is not an option. You are an investor by proxy whether you like it or not. Investment is part of a process that builds the future. The collective results of many decisions made by many people determine the shape of the future that is built.

So how is investment building the future?

Quite literally. An investment is a stock of stuff built up today to provide a flow of services in the future. The present is a stock of stuff – mental and physical. The stock is being continuously modified as we move through time. Sometimes the changes are very fast, sometimes so slow as to be almost imperceptible. An example of very fast change would be the stock of technical knowledge in the computer industry where productivity of silicon chips has doubled every 18 months for many years. An example of very slow change would be in some remote rural areas where agricultural technology based on donkeys and goats has not changed much for thousands of years. Investment sustains and changes the stock of stuff that is carried forwards into the future.

So where is it best to invest?

Well, that depends on what you want to do. Spending time and/ or money is a direct or indirect investment. Most people want to get a return on their time, which is more than simply pecuniary. They want to enjoy what they do, to derive a psychic income if you like. For many people, personal satisfaction takes priority over income maximisation. They work in schools because they like to teach; they do research in universities because they enjoy the pursuit of knowledge.

Let's focus on money for a moment. Where's it best to invest my money?

Investment in the 'gift economy' is about putting time and money into whatever you value. Investing money in the 'market economy' is about getting your money back with a return. It is a bit like banking except the time horizon for an investment may be longer than the time horizon for a loan. The rational economic man invests to get the highest rates of return – qualified by the risk he is taking.

That sounds good. Let's do that!

It is good, but it is not easy. First of all, people are governed as much by their hearts as by their heads. Second, it is hard to know what will give the best rates of return – because they all happen in the future where no one has yet been.

Surely investment is a rational business?

People's investment taste is as varied as the ways in which they spend their time. Often when they invest their money, their judgement is swayed by similar factors. They may be swayed by a brand, simplicity, lack of time, fashion, intrinsic interest, difficulty or social connotations – which may not be compatible with getting the best returns. Even if investors were completely rational, it is not always the case that the people who run businesses in which they invest are completely rational. Countless non-monetary motives slip in: desire to introduce a new product or technology, to employ people, to be recognised, to change an industry, to have the mental satisfaction of being right.

Let's suppose for the sake of argument that we are rational and want to get high returns. How do we do that?

First of all, we have to consider what we mean by a 'return'.

A return is the amount of money we make per unit of capital, per unit of time.

That sounds straightforward. How do we get these returns?

Investments as projects

All investment is about providing capital to some sort of project. Civilisation is a multitude of inter-related projects. People are most familiar with the projects that they go to work on every day.

What sort of work are you in?

I'm a brand manager at an entertainment rights business.

An entertainment rights business? Hmmm. How does that work?

We buy and sell the rights to intellectual property.

How do you make money out of that?

We sell the rights for more than we pay for them.

Okay. How do you explain at an 'idiot boy' level how you do that?

Well, an author creates a character, say Bugs Bunny, or Postman Pat, or Toad of Toad Hall, or Pingu, or Harry Potter. There's a media industry out there which broadcasts on radio and television and makes films, videos and DVDs. The industry needs 'content' to attract and retain the interest of its watchers and listeners. The industry makes money by creating audiences and selling advertisers the right to advertise to those audiences at certain times. We are intermediaries. We intermediate between creative types – authors, who create new 'content', and distributors or media, which wish to show or use the content.

So tell me more about this 'intermediation'.

Well, we find a character or a story or a theme that we like, and we try to work out if and how it will appeal to an audience and exactly what audience. Then we think about the media industry and our contacts and about how they could use the story and through what medium. So, if the story can be serialised as a television show or sold on DVD, we think about how that could be done and how much it would cost. If we think the plot has long-term potential we buy the rights to the story from the author and invest in making the television series. The sort of story we like has such a strong appeal for a particular audience that it can be sold through multiple media channels that reinforce the overall impact. So if the television series works, we commission more books, maybe a film too. And we seek to sell the distribution rights in multiple different geographies.

So how do you know how much to pay for the rights?

Well, it depends whether the story is already well known and already has an audience. If it has an audience then it probably already has distribution deals in place and these will have revenues that we can audit. Somebody will already own these distribution deals. Occasionally these properties come up for sale. We get shown these deals because we are known in the market. The exact amount we pay depends on our view of the revenues and profits which the contracts will generate in the future, how we can add to the revenues by further developing the property or selling it into new channels and, of course, on the negotiation and whether there are other bidders.

And what about the rights to new stories or properties?

These are more difficult to evaluate because there is no track record. The idea has been created, but the product has not yet been built. The distribution contracts have not been signed. The share of mind of the consumer has not been developed.

What you have just described are two sorts of projects – mature projects in which money has already been invested and returns are already being received, and immature projects into which little has yet been invested. At a generic level, most large businesses are portfolios of mature and immature projects.

How do you quantify the amounts you wish to pay for mature projects and immature projects in your business?

For mature projects we can work out how much has been spent on developing the asset, we can examine the contracts that have been signed and see how long they have to run, and what income they are likely to generate. We offer a price that reflects the amount we think that the asset will earn and some premium to reflect the costs that we may be able to save, and the additional contracts or growth that we may be able to add to the asset.

For immature projects the whole process is even more subjective. With a mature project we have precedents. We can see the product, the books, the films, the distribution contracts and so on. We can compare these with the rest of our portfolio. Immature projects are a bit like investing in children. You can never be completely sure how they will turn out.

Immature projects, like children, tend to require continuous investment. And, like children, the time it takes them to become independent and the amount they cost tends to exceed initial expectations!

Are all investments projects?

Investments are all ultimately backed by projects. So it helps to look through to the underlying projects.

The capital supplied to the project usually comes in the form of debt and/or equity. Debt is a loan which is expected to be repaid with interest. Equity is an ownership right which gives the right to participate in any future surpluses generated by the project. Trading in second-hand debt and equity, known as secondary market trading, creates prices.

Projects vary enormously. There are not-for-money projects, not-for-profit projects and commercial projects in the market economy which aim to achieve a financial return on capital.

Which projects prove the most reliable investments?

Mature projects tend to generate cash surpluses. Immature projects consume cash. The ideal investment is a collection of projects in which the mature projects finance the immature. Most successful investment is incremental and cumulative, using or building on what was there before.

Are mature projects less risky than immature projects?

Mature projects are usually more predictable than immature projects. That's because they have been going for some time and have history. But they are not necessarily less risky. Risk depends on many factors including the predictability of the project, for example the price paid for the project and its capital structure.

Tell me about mature projects that let one down.

If you were looking for a reliable investment you might look for the best-known, longest standing organisation you can find, and this might lead you to government and to invest in a government bond. What could be more reliable? It is relatively difficult for a sovereign government to go bust, given that it can create money by issuing bonds and has the right to raise taxes. Yet, on closer examination, one discovers that governments do go bust. They can issue more liabilities than they can raise taxes to repay – and sometimes the liabilities are issued in foreign currencies, which they cannot 'create' as necessary. Argentina issued bonds denominated in US dollars. It had no right to print another country's currency – and it could not repay the bonds on their due dates. Governments can be thought of as organisations and projects in similar fashion to businesses. Government revenues may collapse – particularly if they depend on one industry or commodity. So, for example, in 1998 when the oil price fell to $10 a barrel, the revenues of certain key oil-exporting countries such as Russia also collapsed.

One also discovers that governments have a chronic tendency to let investors down surreptitiously, subtly and slowly over time. They do this when inflation is at, near or greater than the rate of return on money. So, for example, if the cost of the stuff you need to buy in order to live, such as a certain amount of food and fuel, rises in price by 5% per annum and if the value of your capital and your income is fixed, you slowly get poorer. If all your wealth is tied up in a government bond paying you 5% per annum and you spend all of your income then after five years the value of your capital will have fallen by 25% – in fact, by 27.63%, allowing for compounding.

Governments also have great influence over the competitive positioning or comparative advantage of their countries vis-à-vis other countries and this affects the value of their currencies. If the currency you use is devalued and you need to buy a lot of imported goods or goods priced on international markets, your standard of living falls over time. Quite a lot of the 'basic necessities' of modern life are imported. Most of the electricity generated in the UK is produced using coal and gas, most of which is imported; the UK is now a net importer of natural gas and oil, as existing UK reserves decline. So the value of the currency matters. When Harold Wilson's government devalued sterling by 14% in 1967 he said, 'That does not mean, of course, that the pound here in Britain, in your pocket or purse or in your bank, has been devalued.' Unfortunately that is exactly what it meant. People were shocked by the 1967 devaluation. Sterling fell 20–25% against most currencies between 2007 and 2010, but because this happened over several years and because the government is not perceived as being directly responsible, it has not grabbed the same attention.

So you are saying we should not rely on government?

Not entirely. Just that how far you can rely on government depends on your timescale and your view of the future, for example government's ability to meet its liabilities.

When can I rely on investments in immature projects in your analogy?

Immature projects are usually unpredictable unless they have been done before. 'Cutting-edge' projects usually end up taking longer and costing more to reach the stage when they generate cash surpluses. 'Cookie-cutter' projects, or projects which are stamped out according to an existing model, often have a high degree of predictability despite their immaturity.

'And what do you do with these stars?'
'What do I do with them?'
'Yes.'
'Nothing. I own them.'
'You own the stars?'
'Yes.' ...
'And what good does it do you to own the stars?'
'It does me the good of making me rich.'
'And what good does it do you to be rich?'
'It makes it possible for me to buy more stars if any are discovered.' ...
'I myself own a flower,' he continued his conversation with the businessman, 'which I water every day. I own three volcanoes which I clean out every week (for I also clean out the one that is extinct; one never knows). It is of some use to my volcanoes, and it is of some use to my flower, that I own them. But you are no use to the stars.'

The businessman opened his mouth, but he found nothing to say in answer. And the Little Prince went away.

– Antoine de Saint-Exupery, *The Little Prince*

CHAPTER 2

Cash or 'economic' returns versus psychic income

'Everything you learned about the Universe as obvious becomes less and less obvious as you begin to study it.'

– Buckminster Fuller

So how do we get the best returns?

Implicit in the question of how to find the best returns is the question of how to find the best assets. It only sounds simple because we have not explored what we mean by an asset and the different sorts of assets in which we can invest, and because we have not defined what we mean by capital.

In our discussion so far I have just talked about returns in general, as if they are all the same. At risk of 'teaching my grandmother how to suck eggs', I should like to make a minor detour at this point and say a bit more about returns in general. Teaching people how to suck eggs is a risky pastime. I once used this English idiom with an important American woman. She looked daggers at me as if I had uttered an obscenity.

Okay, if you must chase this rabbit down a hole, then you must!

Well, the thing about returns is that people in finance just take them for granted, so to speak. But if you stop to think about it, financial returns are an artificial construct, a product of the economic ecosystem rather than part of the natural ecosystem. There are no laws of Nature that say what returns will be, only some laws of economics, which are usually better at explaining after the event than at predicting.

I sense you are about to complicate things.

We live our lives by over-simplifying everything, but just occasionally it does no harm to re-examine the underlying complexity. Fear not, though; I shall make it as simple as possible but no simpler!

Go on then.

Well, we live in what might be described as a 'highly evolved' financial system. But the building blocks from which it evolved are quite simple. It goes like this. In the beginning, there was 'property' – physical stuff you could claim ownership of. Then came credit – which we can think of as the ability to deliver property in the future. Then came credit in the form of cash – which is a sort of generalised credit that allows 'instant' property transfer within the 'walled garden' of a monetary and banking system. Cash works to transfer property – but only if both parties to the transaction are inside the same system.

How does this help explain 'returns'?

Well, the sort of returns which investors in commercial projects are interested in are all defined in terms of cash. This sounds extremely obvious – but only because we take cash and the banking system for granted. Let me explain. Companies, for example, produce accounts to control their cash and to explain their 'stewardship' of shareholders' assets. What do accounts measure? They really only measure cash.

That does not sound right. When I look at a company balance sheet there's plenty there apart from cash.

That's right. But generically there's only *one* thing in accounts – which is 'assets'. And the only assets in accounts are things which by convention are deemed likely to convert into cash.

We don't even have to consider 'liabilities' as a different class of thing because liabilities are just negative assets. What then are 'assets' for accounting purposes? They are not, as one might naively believe, just 'common or garden' assets. Accountants define assets much more narrowly. To be an accounting asset, a thing must convert into cash with reasonable certainty. Conversion to cash with reasonable certainty is a judgement not a fact, and a probabilistic judgement at that. This is a bit of a shock for people who would like to believe that accounts show 'absolute truth' rather than relative judgement or a best estimate at a given time. Accounts do not measure physical variables like height or weight. They seek to measure cash per unit of time.

But surely most things in accounts convert to cash with reasonable certainty?

But of course! Because they must pass this test to get recorded in the accounts in the first place. Sometimes the assets which do *not* appear in the accounts are as important, or more important, than the assets which qualify as accounting assets.

Accounts are not an inventory of everything a business owns and they do not show its value. A business will own many more things than its accounting assets. It may enjoy the services of brilliant employees, own intellectual property or at least 'know-how', and have valuable relationships with customers and suppliers. But none of these things is directly convertible to cash with reasonable certainty, and hence they are not accounting assets that can be shown in the accounts.

That is a shock! I thought that you could value a business by looking at its accounts.

Well, I was going to complicate things, wasn't I? Yes, you can form a view of a business by looking at its accounts, and yes, the accounts are one of the most useful documents to consider. But it does no harm to remember that accounting value is a subset of economic value, and both are a subset of wider and deeper notions of value.

Value

What exactly is value then?

For the purposes of getting a return the sort of value which one needs to focus on is cash value, of which there are a few variants. One variant is accounting value – which comprises assets (and negative assets, also known as 'liabilities') that are 'on a conveyor belt' on their way to conversion into cash. Accounting assets *exist* at the balance sheet date. We know that because independent auditors have checked – if not every one, then at least all of the 'material' assets and liabilities, and a sample of the rest. But accounting assets are not completely certain to turn into cash. The likelihood of the asset converting into cash depends on the type of asset. The likelihood of the asset being included in the accounts may depend on the aggression or assertiveness of the management.

Another variant of cash value is 'economic value'. Economic value includes accounting assets but it also takes account of assets which do not exist at the balance sheet date, but which are *expected* to be created in the future and discounts them back to the present – the so-called 'present value'.

Accounting and economic assets are all derived from more fundamental, more common or garden assets. We can think of assets that convert into cash at some point as deriving from 'social' assets and 'natural' assets.

So what are 'social' and 'natural' assets?

The word 'social' is just an adjective derived from society. Rather confusingly, the French name for a company is *société*, so a social asset in France has a literal *double entendre*. Social assets are things like languages, which are paradoxically owned by everyone and by no one at the same time. They include knowledge that has not been appropriated by anyone, ideas rather than 'intellectual property', which has a more precise legal definition.

Natural assets are natural phenomena. When these have not been appropriated by anyone – a natural person or a legal person like a state, they are notionally owned in common, the natural heritage of all mankind. Once a natural asset – such as an ore body or a coalfield or an oilfield – has been appropriated by someone it becomes an economic asset – that is, it has an economic value because it is expected to generate cash.

Hmmm, now aren't you over-complicating things? Surely the value of something is ultimately what it cost to produce?

Yes, economics does try to persuade us that something's value is related to its cost of production. The argument goes that if supply and demand are not constrained, the effect of competition will reduce prices to a level where the 'factors' of production – labour, natural resources and financial and real capital – are all adequately, but only adequately, compensated. In other words cost equates with value.

Like many economic theories this one is intellectually appealing but also dangerous. Dangerous because it does not work all the time and it leaves out inherently difficult and subjective factors. For example, we are less confident than our 19th-century ancestors that the economic ecosystem adequately prices the cost of natural resources. The negative side effects of exploiting some natural resources may not be in the price at all. Carbon emissions are one of the biggest side effects of modern civilisation's use of hydrocarbons to generate energy. But the economic ecosystem has never adequately priced these emissions.

Another difficult subjective element is 'demand'. What causes people to demand what they demand? Demand for many products is not a given, an exogenous variable. Desire is expressly manufactured for some products. An extreme example of this is diamonds. Gem diamonds are sublimely useless. Advertising has created demand for gem diamonds by exploiting psychology. What does economics do when people desire the wrong things? Whole societies have devoted colossal resources to enterprises we would now regard as mad, like the Pyramids in Egypt. What if the Pharaohs had devoted the same resources to something more productive? Modern satirists wonder about the sustainability and 'productivity' of some wars and some economic 'development'.

But on the whole you accept that cost and value tend to converge?

Sometimes, perhaps most of the time, but not always. Although supply and demand for some commodities may sometimes reach some theoretical equilibrium, for most things supply and demand are deflected by changes in technology, substitutes, regulation and raw material prices. Cost and value may be out of synch most of the time.

Cost and price and value are ephemeral and subjective things. Theoretical economic cost is one point on the compass. It helps us navigate but it is not enough.

Time can be a significant element in value. If a machine is operating at full capacity and is mission critical to an entire system then the 'value' of a spare part shipped to arrive within hours may be a multiple of cost. The same spare part might trade below cost if the machine has been superseded or if there is excess capacity. Penicillin for someone dying of pneumonia is almost priceless because it may save a life. But capital and know-how are the only constraints on the production of penicillin and so as a stock item in a warehouse penicillin is worth little more than its cost of production. Why does some art trade at exotic multiples of cost? The time and materials which Van Gogh put in to create his still lives, *Sun Flowers* or *Irises*, cost a minute fraction of the value paid for these pictures at auction decades after his death. Economics attributes the price premium commanded by a Van Gogh over other artists to scarcity. Does the buyer of the picture believe that he is buying a scarce resource or some quintessence of life?

So what else do we need?

Cost and value are opposite sides of the same coin. After all, one person's cost is another person's value. But they are not the same. We need to recognise the difficulties created by time.

Value is a forward-looking concept. Economic value is the present value of the cash surpluses which an asset will generate in the future. Cost is a backwards-looking concept. It is the cash that was spent to produce the item – the price paid at a point in time or the historic cost of production. The definition of economic value is *ex ante* and the definition of cost is *ex post*. The *ex ante* expectation of the cost may be quite different from the *ex post* realisation. For example, some costs may not emerge for generations, they may accrue to someone other than the manufacturer and they might be very difficult to quantify in terms of cash. The cost of making and using some forms of asbestos is an example.

Are you saying that the cost of something is not objective then?

Cost, like value, can be a tricky concept. The tricky step is the conversion of some 'real' thing into a monetary amount. In the economic value system 'cost' and 'value' are made up of cash costs or money's worth costs. The tricky bit is what *is* the value or cost of something that pre-exists the money value or cost. What does it cost to have an idea? What is the cost or value of a coal seam? What is the cost or value of a river? What is the cost or value of a language?

So can you give me an example of a cost that is not 'objective'?

Suppose you are inspired by something to believe that the existence of a given protein in blood predicts lung cancer. And suppose you test it and it is true. Your idea has a cost – which is all your experiences up to the point of inspiration. But what is this cost? How do we value this cost? The practical *test* of the idea has a *cash* cost – and that's much easier to quantify in terms of money. The idea itself has no directly attributable cash cost.

Suppose we believe that the cost of your idea is approximately zero – because you spent no cash to create the idea; because, in the larger scheme of things, it is, so to speak, 'God-given'? This has implications. One implication might be that you cannot own your idea, that society will not grant you property rights over your idea. In that case, your idea may have much lower financial value to you, although you may still enjoy pride of 'authorship' rather than the fruits of 'ownership'. Indeed, you might not feel any incentive to commercialise your idea. You might 'take it with you' to your grave!

Another implication is that if the idea is made widely available and is freely exploited, the costs of testing for this protein will fall to somewhere close to the cost of producing the test. Given economies of scale, the costs might fall to extremely low levels.

Are all costs the same?

Of course, the economic and accounting system reduces everything to a money price and makes everything comparable in money terms. This creates the impression that all costs are the same. But no, costs are not all the same. There are cash costs and non-cash costs. There are the costs borne by the buyer of the service and there may be 'externalities' – costs borne by third parties.

E.F. Schumacher[3] considered that natural resources were 'extra-economic assets', outside the economic ecosystem, as it were. He considered that it was an economic myth that a barrel of oil is 'free' beyond its financial cost of production or beyond society's willingness to buy it. Schumacher argued that hydrocarbons were natural capital, a stock to be maintained rather than income to be spent. He believed that civilisation is spending its hydrocarbon 'inheritance' profligately without providing for its 'replacement cost'. Civilisation does not have an answer to the question, what will happen when hydrocarbons run out? Politicians either deny the premise (it will never happen) or express faith in technological progress (something will come up).

Cost can be as elusive as value. Costs ought to include a component for the cost of supplying capital. Capital is often a non-cash cost, or a cost borne by someone else, or a historic cost paid decades past. Capital includes natural, social and financial capital. Many natural assets are not priced at all. Many social assets may not have any direct costs – only indirect costs like taxes. Surprisingly, even some forms of financial capital have no explicit cost! Equity capital is an ownership right rather than a financial claim. At one level the cost of equity is just like all costs and all value – it can be determined in cash terms. At a less superficial level the 'cost'

---

[3] E.F. Schumacher, *Small Is Beautiful*, 1973.

of equity has similar philosophical difficulties as the cost of owning a beautiful river or an oil reservoir.

Does this get us anywhere?

I think it gets us to a point where we need to accept what a difficult concept value is. Economic and accounting systems do not really address the question of value. All they do is create systems for pricing.

I suppose value is a bit like energy. Everyone experiences it. It can be defined and measured in certain circumstances. But no one knows what it actually *is*. Ultimately, value is like great art, priced and priceless.

In making this sally into the territory of 'value' and 'cost', I've heard myself using words like 'cash', 'capital', 'equity', 'debt' and 'return'. I have not really defined value at all – I've just applied these different labels to it. We use these labels so often that their meaning is lost behind a 'veil of obviousness'. All these words are from the world of 'market exchange'. They define 'value' in specific ways which, from a broader perspective, can be seen as arbitrary simplifications of reality. The economic ecosystem is in the business of producing prices for different things. It does this without really knowing what value is. Indeed, its concept of value changes across time. For example, carbon emissions had no price/cost until 'cap and trade' systems were introduced.

Economic cost, like economic value, comes and goes. Both are ephemeral, at least from a longer historical perspective.

Does that mean we have to look to the gift economy to find 'intrinsic value'?

How different it all is in the world of 'gift exchange'. The founder of the first girls' school in Korea, an American missionary, gave it the motto, 'Truth, Goodness, and Beauty'. She too was describing 'value', but from a different perspective, using a different vocabulary!

If we want to find 'permanent' value, we have to look beyond real assets or financial assets or economic costs or value to the great ineffable – spiritual value. It's there, whether or not it is noticed, and in business it is often the case that people are just too busy to take notice.

Poetry rather than prices capture the ineffable:

> *A thing of beauty is a joy for ever:*
> *Its loveliness increases; it will never*
> *Pass into nothingness; but still will keep*
> *A bower quiet for us, and a sleep*
> *Full of sweet dreams, and health, and quiet breathing.*[4]

Oh dear! The conversation has taken a metaphysical turn.

Well, the physical and the metaphysical can be difficult to separate! Paradox is at the heart of all truth. In the final analysis, there's no getting away from the metaphysical in economics because all value depends on credit, belief in the future. A financial asset like cash has no intrinsic value. It has value because whoever takes it in exchange expects it to have equivalent value when he exchanges the cash again in the future. A real asset has value because people believe it will generate profits or have a re-sale value.

So what is 'intrinsic value' in the exchange economy?

There's a 'textbook' answer to this question and it is that intrinsic value – in an economic sense – is the present value of future cash surpluses.

---

[4] John Keats, extract from 'Endymion', Book 1, published in 1818.

The textbook answer is very general. The thing about present value numbers is that they are one-number summaries of collections of cash surpluses that may stretch over many years. The same one-number summary 'present value' may represent a huge variety of different cashflow streams – all having different profiles over time.

When value investors talk of 'intrinsic value', they really mean a 'present value' figure where all or most of the value can be found in the present or in the very near term cash surpluses, rather than in cash surpluses which are expected to be generated five or ten or fifteen years out. Ben Graham's[5] tests of value related to accounting assets that could be found on a balance sheet.

Time, capital and income

> *'What the economist calls 'capital' is nothing more than human knowledge imposed on the material world. Knowledge and the growth of knowledge, therefore, is the essential key to economic development. Investment, financial systems and economic organisations and institutions are in a sense only the machinery by which a knowledge process is created and expressed.'*
>
> – Kenneth E. Boulding

So, now you've raised the question of time.

Yes, we need to consider the importance of time in investment. It is rather fundamental.

A return is the amount of money we make per unit of capital, *per unit of time.*

---

[5] Benjamin Graham (1894–1976) was an American economist and professional investor.

This is a circular definition. Capital is defined by time; it is a stock rather than a flow. And it only has a value because it can be consumed in some way in the future! So we have to try to figure out how time fits in.

Okay, so why is time so important?

All of investment is an attempt to defeat the forces of time!

When one stands back from it, investment is about creating and sustaining a way of life. A one-word summary is 'civilisation'. Investment creates civilisation. The whole system of civilisation is geared to harnessing real assets and getting them to produce a flow of resources at the times when they are needed. Civilisation is about creating capabilities and sustaining them across time. To do this, civilisation exploits stocks of resources, natural and human, and turns them into a flow of consumable products. Early or late delivery of the product results in disruption: the planes/trains/ships depart late, the electric lights go off, factories close, jobs are lost, debt is written off.

Give me an example of capital being deployed to provide a future capability.

Take electricity. To supply electricity, physical stocks of natural assets must be found and made available, for example, coal or gas or uranium or water. A stock of capacity, human and physical, must be created to process these raw materials. The natural resources must then be run through the generating capacity to produce the electricity as and when required. All of this requires planning to gather the resources and the capacity so that the electricity is available at the right time. To manage the process, time must be cut up into discrete units, typically years and months, or, in the case of electricity, into half hours or even smaller units.

So how are the 'capabilities' put together to deliver the right flow of product per unit of time?

The capabilities are brought together by the 'economic ecosystem', which depends on inter-dependent legal, accounting and economic concepts. Among these are the notions of 'capital' and 'income'. Time defines capital and income. Capital is a stock of resources or 'capability' at a moment of time. Income is a flow of resources or product per unit of time. In the long run an investment return is the flow of income that derives from capital. The flow of income results from using the capital to create the capability to supply some product to some customer.

So how is it that a collection of 'costs' can create a 'return' – in other words, pay back more cash than they cost to buy?

There's a certain amount of alchemy about this! Just how is it possible to get more out than is put in?

One way of looking at it is to ask whether there's an equivalent in economics to the notion of the conservation of matter in physics. In physics, energy and matter in a closed system can be transformed but not created. If it appears as if matter has been created, it is because there's been an error in the measurement of the inputs and outputs.

Economic systems are *not* closed in a number of important respects. Most fundamentally, they receive daily sustainable energy from the Sun in the form of sunlight or solar energy. They also take resources from natural systems without rigorously measuring their costs in terms of the degradation of the environment. They take resources from neighbouring economies through the use and abuse of bargaining power, forms, if you like, of implicit or explicit 'colonialism'. And they take resources from the future by creating credit, claims on the future.

Growth in income, either at the level of an individual corporation or at the level of an entire economy, has many possible causes. Greater efficiency might have allowed more output to be created with the same input – an improvement in productivity. Or, the increase in output may have been caused by using more inputs – natural, social, human or financial. There are several ways of increasing inputs that are not always rigorously measured. One way is to bring more resources into the economic ecosystem by simply appropriating more natural resources. Another way is to go out and conquer other civilisations – a strategy implicitly or explicitly pursued by most empires. Another is to create financial capital – to borrow. Borrowing is moving resources across time – borrowing from the future to deploy resources in the present. If the true cost of the additional natural, social and financial capital introduced were measured, it might be the case that the increase in income was illusory.

And what do you mean by capital?

Well, the simplest way of looking at capital is as a stock or accumulation of 'stuff' at a point in time. The stuff is a resource or a capability. What makes the stuff 'capital' is that it endures over several periods of time. Income, by contrast, is stuff that is produced or consumed within a period of time.

Sunlight is income because it is a flow; it cannot be directly put into a bottle and stocked. Coal or oil are capital because they are stocks of energy which can be used in the future. The origin of the energy is in fact sunlight captured by plants and animals and stored by geological and chemical processes.

In order to appropriate stuff from Nature, ownership rights must be created. Resources become someone's property. As soon as the concept of ownership exists, there is a separation of the 'right' or 'claim' to the property from the property itself. This creates two sorts of capital which are the opposite sides of the same coin: financial capital based on the ownership right, and real or physical capital based on the thing itself. 'Real' capital and financial capital have a symbiotic relationship – each creates the other. Financial capital coordinates and organises physical capital.

A 'product' is a good or a service delivered at the right place and time. In order to make it possible to deliver a product, physical and financial capital must be built up, run down and replenished. There are natural systems where the physical replenishment of the stock takes place 'naturally', without human intervention. A river or a lake will sustain itself if the rate of extraction of water or fish stays within limits or is regulated. In economic systems, most products require continued investment in real and financial assets in order to sustain the flow of product.

Is capital necessary to capitalism?

Capital is essential to our civilisation and to life! Capital is just a stock. It takes many forms. There's natural capital – at a macro level in the form of the natural ecosystem and at a micro level in the form of stocks of fresh water, or coal or farmland. There's human capital – the stock of knowledge/experience/skill that is built up by people and organisations. There's man-made physical capital in the form of infrastructure like roads and equipment like capital goods.

And there's financial capital, which is a representation of the physical capital. It is a stock of credit that is supported by ownership claims on existing stocks of natural and man-made physical stocks, and by contracts, which command the future use of human and physical capital.

It is impossible to live without capital in some form. The most fundamental form is the natural environment – which can be thought of as a stock of natural capital. Some civilisations operate almost entirely on the basis of this stock of natural capital. The Amondawa tribe, who were 'discovered' by the outside world in 1986 and who live in the Amazon on the border between Brazil and Bolivia, are a surviving example. Anthropologists from the University of Portsmouth report that the Amondawa language and culture has a very different concept of time. They have no words for week, month or year, and do not think of future time as something which can be measured, counted or talked about in the abstract.

If capital is so essential, why is capitalism vilified?

The issue is partly one of power and control, and partly psychology.

What are the power and control problems of capitalism?

There's a lot of fighting over who gets their hands on the steering wheel. It is an age-old problem. The ancient Greeks characterised it as the struggle between different systems of government – tyranny, oligarchy, and democracy. Modern politics has it as a struggle between socialism and capitalism.

There are some substantive differences of policy – but these have diminished over time. Control is to a significant degree determined by ownership structures. Once upon a time, socialism demanded government ownership of all the means of production. Private ownership was considered inefficient, particularly in the 1930s when levels of unemployment were very high.

Government ownership is pervasive in most economies. But government control over the means of production is no longer regarded as necessarily more efficient, even by self-declared socialists.

Friedrich von Hayek[6] pointed out the risks to freedom that arise if government owns all the means of production. He argued that widely spread ownership and a system which defended private ownership was a bulwark against tyranny.

Does capitalism have a psychological problem?

Well, if capitalism is a mindset which thinks about time as finite and subdivided and slices resources up into units of consumption per unit of time then it is not difficult to see how this can become a psychological problem if it becomes a mono-mania!

Is this a 'natural' way of thinking? The unconscious human mind may think of the world as timeless, more like the Amondawa Indians' way of thinking. The modern conscious mind worries about time, being 'on time', 'saving time', 'wasting time'.

Carl Jung said,

> 'Separation from his instinctual nature inevitably plunges civilized man into a conflict between conscious and unconscious, spirit and nature, knowledge and faith, a split that becomes pathological the moment his consciousness is no longer able to neglect or suppress his instinctual side.'[7]

Satire is how many of these conflicts are expressed. One of the greatest political satires of the 20th century, *Animal Farm*,[8] is an allegory which shows the corrupting effects of power on laudable ideals. Another 20th-century satire, *Modern Times*,[9] is a plea for a different set of values than so-called economic efficiency.

---

[6] Friedrich August von Hayek (1899–1992) was a Nobel laureate in economics, a social scientist and a political theorist.

[7] Jung, Carl (2006). *The Undiscovered Self: The Problem of the Individual in Modern Society*. New American Library.

[8] *Animal Farm*, written by George Orwell, was first published in 1945.

[9] *Modern Times*, the 1936 film written and produced by Charlie Chaplin.

So how, in practical terms, is investment 'defeating the forces of time'?

Businesses move resources across time. 'Non-financial corporations', defined so as to exclude banks, take employees' time and suppliers' raw materials and use them to build longer-term real assets, physical or 'real' capital. These real assets create systems for delivering goods and services to customers. These systems include very long maturity infrastructure assets like railways, ports and airports, long maturity capital goods like power stations and buildings, and medium maturity assets like trucks and IT systems. They also include the product of the education system, capable human beings, which can be thought of as 'human capital'.

Financial corporations create money and bank credit. Banks create short maturity financial liabilities and bank deposits, and co-create longer-term financial assets like loans to customers. The long-term loans help customers to accumulate the resources to build up longer-term real assets.

The activity of creating short-term financial liabilities and using them to create longer-term financial assets is known as 'maturity transformation'. All economic units engage in 'maturity transformation' in some fashion. Transforming the maturity of financial assets is a speciality of the banking system. Transferring the maturity of real assets is the speciality of non-financial businesses.

And does the economic ecosystem succeed in defeating the forces of time?

Only time will tell! The lessons of history are that economic ecosystems succeed for much of the time, but also that they periodically fail. A broad measure of success is 'civilisation', however defined. A narrower measure of success is the creation of 'income'. Failure takes many forms and has many causes.

Common forms of failure include inflation, which is a chronic form of default on debt; high unemployment; government bankruptcy; or the collapse of the monetary system. The currencies of most countries have collapsed at various points in the last hundred years.

So how is 'income' a measure of the success of the economic ecosystem?

The economic definition of income, attributed to the English economist Sir John Hicks, is the amount you can consume without being worse off.

This definition requires some measure of capital at the beginning and end of each period. It also requires income to be measured in 'real' rather than 'nominal' or money terms.

Since 1945 governments have measured and reported on their national incomes. Measuring income is difficult – particularly the aggregate income of a defined economic 'zone'. To make an estimate of aggregate income, use is made of the insight that, in the aggregate, everyone's income must equal everyone's spending, which must equal what everyone produces. So income, spending and production are estimated separately and sort of 'triangulated' to find out where we are.

In practice, what gets measured is production, and the particular measure which is regularly estimated and published is Gross Domestic Product (GDP). It is a bit easier to collect regular figures for production because most production of goods and services is done by corporations, and corporations usually dutifully provide financial and other information to government. GDP is 'gross' because it is before any cost of capital depletion.

The whole system is very imperfect. The capital used by the economy – natural capital, for example – is only imperfectly measured. Changes to national wealth caused by the discovery, production and depletion of natural resources like oil fields are only indirectly captured.

There is a rather large problem with measuring income and capital. It is that financial capital is only a representation of physical capital. Financial capital follows the laws of mathematics, in particular compound interest. Physical capital follows the laws of physics, in particular entropy. Whereas financial capital theoretically compounds indefinitely, physical capital wastes away.

What do you mean by that? Why does financial capital follow mathematical law and real capital physical law?

What I mean is that a financial asset or financial capital (not including equity, which we can treat as a real rather than a financial asset) is governed by contract and by mathematical formulae. Debt capital does not of itself deteriorate or rot in the way a real asset deteriorates. It grows by compound interest.

The real asset side of balance sheets follows physical laws. Real assets are difficult to put together and they fall apart relatively more easily. The component physical assets wear out and the project structures which contain the physical assets, the organisations and their legal and social structures also require human energy to keep them together. This is a bit like the second law of thermodynamics which states that energy in a closed system will only flow from hot to cold; that entropy or disorder always increases; that in a closed system with no additional energy physical processes flow in one direction only.

Much of finance is based on the mathematics of compound interest. Economics takes compound interest, the notion that money grows in value over time as interest is credited, and uses it in reverse. It says that future money can be 'discounted back to the present' at some interest rate. Most mathematical processes are time independent – they work forwards and backwards and just as well in each direction.

The financial side of the balance sheet works according to mathematical law – all else being equal, it is supposed to grow and shrink symmetrically according to formulae. The financial side of balance sheets shrink when the real assets fail to 'live up to expectations'!

Most forms of physical capital suffer deterioration over time – which one might loosely describe as the effect of entropy. Gold is a rare exception – and even gold costs money to protect and to store, even if it does not deteriorate. Human capital also wears out – as generations die out and new generations need to be trained up. In all of this it may be that only intellectual capital has negative entropy – negentropy.

For most of human history compound interest only really applied to debt. Now, in modern financial theory, even equity capital is deemed to have a 'required rate of return' – which reflects its opportunity costs and risks.

An example would help!

Well, the classic financial asset is a bond. A bond is just a legal contract and the particular terms that are put into the bond are, to a large extent, arbitrary. The interest rate that accrues is the result of negotiating power and market alternatives. And the return to the bond holder follows mathematical law. For compound interest to apply, a bond is usually 'insulated' from reality to some extent. Insulated in the sense that the bond holder will require the bond issuer to provide a buffer or excess of income over interest payable and a buffer of assets over the capital value of the bond.

An equity is an indirect ownership interest in a collection of real assets arranged in a business model that is owned by a company. It does not promise any particular rate of return.

A bond contract essentially promises to return capital with interest. Other financial assets are more complicated contracts.

A 'final salary' pension is a promise to pay an annuity income for the remainder of someone's life after they have retired. The amount of the annuity may depend on a variety of factors – like the individual's 'final' salary, and the subsequent rate of wage inflation.

The explicit promises in a final salary pension ultimately confront physical realities – the main one being how long the pensioner lives. This longevity risk has generally been underestimated and has driven some pension schemes into reneging on their promises.

And what about economic law?

Economics operates at the 'intersection' of legal law, accounting law, mathematical law and physical law! The joke goes that it suffers from 'physics envy'! It's a good joke because it is partly true. Economists want to be 'taken seriously' by finding laws with the same sort of predictive powers as physics. If physics can put men on the Moon, why can't economics create full employment, health, fulfilment and happiness? Unfortunately, economic reality is rather messy. It is where human models and aspirations confront physical and psychological reality.

And what about legal law and accounting law?

Physics and mathematics are models of 'natural' phenomena. The phenomena usually pre-exist the models. The phenomena are 'objective'. If the models do not fit the phenomena they are put aside or superseded. If the models fit they are treated as physical and mathematical laws – true in all circumstances or all usual or defined circumstances.

Legal law has a kernel of 'natural' law that is considered to follow natural phenomena. The natural 'kernel' may include rules such as that mothers will look after their children, or that 'thou shalt not kill'. But most legal law is a convention agreed upon to make civilisation work. It is debatable whether even laws that are enshrined in Moses's Ten Commandments, such as 'Thou shalt not steal', are 'ordained by nature' or 'objective' or 'absolute' in the same way as the laws of thermodynamics. Theft presupposes property and vice versa. Property may exist in nature – for example, animals defend territory – but it does not apply everywhere on the planet in exactly the same way like many physical laws. Lawyers and governments routinely define property and re-allocate ownership – sometimes upon a whim.

Accounting rules, like legal rules, are also a convention agreed upon to make civilisation work. At its heart, accounting really only counts cash or things that are expected to turn into cash. Complicated rules have been created to turn cash into real and financial 'capital' and into 'income', so that smoothed cash surpluses can be matched to time periods. But the net of all these rules is that ultimately a profit is just a cash surplus.

The accounting profession has been asked to do more and more. Once upon a time, it just counted the pennies. Then it elaborated the counting to allow for real and financial capital. Then it came up with progressively more sophisticated ways of matching the usage of financial and real capital to specific accounting periods to create consistent profit figures. Then it started to try to value assets and produce 'meaningful' balance sheets. The world would like accounting to value real assets rather than just put them down at cost. The pinnacle of expectations has been reached now that people are looking for measures of 'performance'. This is all very laudable. But there is a limit to what it is possible for accounts to achieve. What might theoretically be achievable may be impractical.

Some people in society affect to despise or really despise commerce and accounting and even money. Some of them may consider that they have a more refined or artistic appreciation of the meaning of life! But paradox applies and they are not completely wrong all the time. It is as well to recognise that there are circumstances in which a cash profit, or an accounting profit, do not coincide with the ideal or Platonic profit.

Social, natural and economic assets. 'Real' assets and financial assets

Let's get back to returns. How do I get a return on my money by buying assets?

Ah yes, as I was saying, you have to buy assets, and the sort of asset you buy determines what sort of return you can expect to get. You could buy a 'social' or a 'natural' asset. You might buy a work of art or a stretch of river or a football club. The financial returns from these assets may be very low – because the revenue-generating capability of the assets might be low or non-existent. But you might derive enormous satisfaction from owning these sorts of assets, and if you discover a modern-day Van Gogh you, or your heirs, might get unjustly rewarded by huge capital appreciation!

Are you saying that there's no point in investing in social or natural assets?

It depends on what sort of return you want to make. If you want a psychic income or social income, which are not to be sniffed at, then social and natural assets are an appropriate investment.

Most investors want and need returns – which must ultimately arrive in money's worth – and they need them on a shortish time horizon, like within their lifetime. Some people are philanthropists and some organisations like governments must consider multi-generational time horizons. But most people need to have returns.

You have asked where we find the best returns. Getting the best returns at an acceptable level of risk within an acceptable time frame usually involves some compromise. We need to get a return today derived from economic assets that will produce cash surpluses, and on an 'economic' or shortish time horizon. But the economic assets of today were once the uneconomic social and natural assets of yesterday. So it makes sense to have economic assets with some optionality, some potential to create future economic value.

So it is not an 'either/or' choice between economic assets and social or natural assets?

Definitely not. Economic assets all derive from social and natural assets. You can't have one without the other. The thing about social and natural assets is that they may be convertible into economic assets at some point. But in order to turn a social asset into an economic asset, some sort of business model must be applied to the asset. It might take a hundred years for someone to find a business model, to exercise the conversion 'option', as it were, or it might take five years. When Michael Faraday discovered electro-magnetic induction, the physics of generating electricity, he discovered a real asset, a natural phenomenon, which he could encapsulate in ideas. This real asset had no economic value for Faraday since he never patented or sold his ideas. And yet this 'real option' has been progressively exercised by other people in society over the subsequent 150-odd years and been applied in a variety of different business models. Electricity is now considered a 'normal' requirement of civilisation.

Education is a classic example of a social asset. Education is about acquiring knowledge and skills that are real assets. Two people can receive the same education and end up in completely different economic circumstances. One might be a cash-strapped university lecturer. Another might be a 'loaded' entrepreneur. Or a loaded university lecturer and a cash-strapped entrepreneur! Education is an 'option' which the educated person implicitly exercises over the course of a lifetime.

So the highest priority is to buy 'economic assets'?

Yes, assets which are expected to generate a cash value at some point. In the jargon of modern financial economics, the Holy Grail is 'economic value'. Economic value involves some difficult concepts: it requires a measure of the value of the assets employed, and measures of some normative or subjective 'required' rate of return and of the actual cash return. The source of economic value is an 'economic asset'. Economic assets fall into two main categories: there are real assets and there are financial assets.

You'll have to explain the distinction between a 'real' and a 'financial' asset

Okay. Real assets could be broadly described as 'real stuff', property, if you like, other than money and financial assets. What constitutes property has changed over time. There is no fixed class of stuff which constitutes property. Its composition differs in different jurisdictions and over time. Property includes the realm of ideas. Some ideas which have specific and novel applications can be patented and are a form of property in their own right. New knowledge, whether or not patented, creates the potential for new forms of property. For example, a new process for separating alumina made bauxite valuable property. After nuclear fission was invented, uranium ceased being an economically worthless chemical element and became a valuable raw material for nuclear power stations. A computer game is a type of property that did not exist before computers.

Some property endures for a long time but most property wastes away – like a natural resource or a copyright – although the rate of decay varies. It would be comforting if there were some property which represented some fixed value. Some people think of gold as having a permanent value. In a physical sense, gold is about as permanent a form of stuff as can be found since it does not corrode. There about 170,000 tonnes of gold in the world and all the gold ever mined still exists. In a financial sense, the value of gold varies considerably over time. Its cost of production is a function of the richness of the ore deposits that are being mined and the cost of energy – for which the price of oil is a proxy. Gold is often used as money – and the value of gold varies greatly with faith in the banking system. The price of gold rises in nominal terms as the real value of money declines.

And what do you mean by financial assets?

Financial assets are defined in terms of amounts of money. A typical financial asset is a bond – a contract to deliver a fixed amount of money. The amount and nature of the financial assets in an economy is not fixed but varies in time and place.

Real Assets

'At particular times a great deal of stupid people have a great deal of stupid money... At intervals... the money of these people – the blind capital, as we call it, of the country – is particularly large and craving; it seeks for someone to devour it, and there is a 'plethora'; it finds someone and there is 'speculation'; it is devoured, and there is panic.'

– Walter Bagehot

'You can talk about socialising your railways and other things, socialise credit and the rest is comparatively easy.'

– Aneurin Bevan, 1931

'Because it is through the limitation of our money incomes that we feel the restrictions which our relative poverty still imposes on us, many have come to hate money as the symbol of these restrictions. Actually, money is one of the greatest instruments of freedom ever invented by man. It is money which in existing society opens an astounding range of choice to the poor man – a range greater than that which not many generations ago was open to the wealthy.'

– Friedrich von Hayek

'Banks have done more injury to the religion, morality, tranquility, prosperity and even wealth of the nation than they can have done or ever will do good.'

– President John Adams, 1819

CHAPTER 3

Money, financial assets and 'real' assets

'Credit: Man's Confidence in Man' 'Credit is the vital air of the system of modern commerce. It has done more – a thousand times more – to enrich nations than all the mines of the world.'[10]

– John Moody

Beautiful credit! The foundation of modern society. Who shall say that this is not the golden age of mutual trust, of unlimited reliance upon human promises?[11]

– Mark Twain

And doesn't that beg the question, 'What is money?'

Yes. Financial assets are defined in terms of money. So I have not satisfactorily defined a financial asset if I cannot tell you what money is.

---

[10] John Moody, who founded Moody's, the credit rating agency, in 1913, had these words inscribed on a bronze inscription installed over the door of the new office building he commissioned in 1951 together with the quote from US Senator Daniel Webster below it.

[11] Mark Twain, *The Gilded Age*. The passage continues: 'That is a peculiar condition of society which enables a whole nation to instantly recognize point and meaning in the familiar newspaper anecdote, which puts into the mouth of a distinguished speculator in lands and mines this remark: "I wasn't worth a cent two years ago, and now I owe two millions of dollars."'

So can you define money?

Yes – whereas some things defy real definition, money, being a purely human construct, can be defined. Phenomena like 'energy' or 'time' are defined in terms of what they do, but what they are remains a mystery. Money can be defined in terms of what it is as well as what it does.

Money is a specialised form of credit. Credit is a contract to deliver something in the future. The word derives from the Latin *credo,* to believe. In the case of credit, future repayment or delivery of 'value' is the thing believed in. Just as it takes two hands to clap, it requires two parties to create credit. Everyone gives and receives credit. You take credit from your utility suppliers – for your electricity, water, gas and telephone supplies, for example. You give credit to your employer when you work for a month before getting paid.

There are many different forms of credit. Money is just a specialised form of credit – the credit of the banking system. Money and bank credit are created simultaneously by banks when they lend to customers: a loan to a customer creates bank credit – which is money owed *to* the bank – and creates money in the form of a bank deposit – which is money owed *by* the bank.

The credit of the banking system is created at two levels: cash, which is a liability of the central bank; and deposits, which are the liability of commercial banks. Money is in many respects a government-created product in that the creation of *cash* is a monopoly of the central bank, which is owned by the State. The central bank creates cash, which it uses to buy assets. The value of the cash derives both from the value of the assets that the central bank buys, and from the credit of the government as the main shareholder of the central bank.

Commercial banks 'collateralise' central bank money in the sense that they create financial assets (bank deposits) which are claims to cash or central bank money. Commercial banks 'manufacture' loans and deposits.

Deposits are a derivative. They are valuable because they can be converted into cash. Deposits are pretty much universally accepted as money within a monetary system – in other words, within a country like the UK or within a currency zone such as the euro zone.

Commercial banks co-create credit with their customers when they lend to them. Bank credit is the loan due *to* the bank. Money is the equal and opposite deposit the bank creates in the name of the borrower – money owed to the borrower by the bank.

Once upon a time, cash was gold and deposits were a 'warehouse warrant', giving the holder the right to go to the warehouse and claim their gold. Now deposits are just the collateralised asset base of the commercial banking system and cash is the collateralised asset base of the central bank – backed by the credit of the central government.

I find it difficult to visualise the relationship of money with credit. Can you simplify it for me?

Well they say a picture is worth a thousand words. So I can draw you a picture to represent the relationships. Here it is:

Money vs Credit

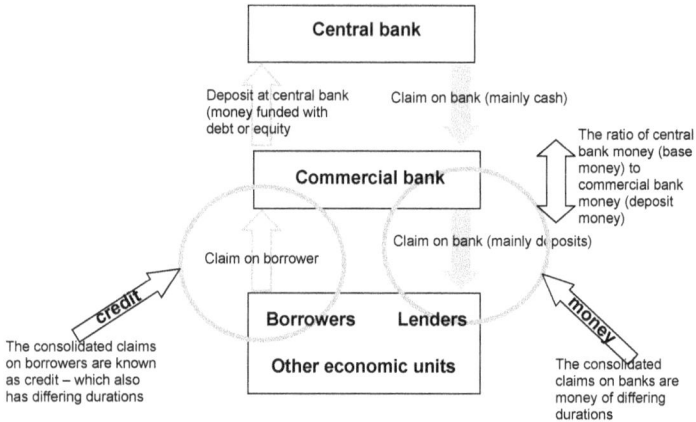

The picture is of course a simplification. But it distinguishes between the main types of money – central bank money or cash and commercial bank money or deposits. It also shows how the value of money and the value of credit are reflexive. In modern systems money is not 'redeemable' in some real commodity like gold. Money is worth what it has been spent on – which is credit. If society as a whole has spent the credit on less and less productive things then both credit and money will depreciate to reflect the longer term productivity of the system.

So what is the relationship between the value of 'real' assets and the value of financial assets?

The value of real and financial assets is reflexive. Financial assets ultimately derive their value from real assets. And the real assets are implicitly and explicitly being valued by the financial assets.

You talk about the value of financial assets deriving from real assets. Do you mean that they are derivatives?

Derivatives are things which derive their value from other variables. The variety of financial instruments has multiplied over time. Financial derivatives – options, futures and swaps – have been created on a wide range of real and financial assets. Many forms of assets have been securitised – that is, used as security for financial assets – for example mortgage loans, trade receivables and commodities.

You can have derivatives on derivatives on derivatives. So a call option on a stock exchange index – for example, the right to buy the FTSE 100 index at a certain price over a defined future period – is a legal right which derives its value from the level of the index. The level of the index in turn derives its value from the underlying equity shares which make up the index. The underlying equity shares derive their value from the business projects which underlie the equity shares.

Derivatives can derive their value from real or financial assets. But at the end of the chain there are real assets arranged in some business model or another. Ultimately, one can think of government as a form of business model organizing real assets.

Derivatives can be difficult to value. The key input into the valuation model may be a market price. So the validity of the valuation may depend on the continued availability of a market price. If the relevant market closes or if volumes dries up, the valuation model has to be re-assessed.

One can think of derivatives as froth on the stream of real assets and liabilities.

Talk about complicated!

Yes, derivatives can get extremely complicated. An analogy may help to put them in context. Suppose you own a racehorse. Ownership of the horse is equity. A loan secured on the horse is a financial liability/asset. A bet on whether the horse will win specific races is a derivative contract.

Or to take the analogy up a level, suppose you own a racecourse. Ownership of the racecourse is equity. Loans secured on the property are debt. A contract which pays out depending on the number of races cancelled by reason of bad weather is a derivative.

It makes sense for some people to own derivatives. A racecourse owner could buy a weather-related derivative contract in order to hedge the risk of bad weather. A market maker could run a book of weather derivative contracts and thereby allow its counterparties to manage their weather risk exposure better. The derivative contracts are a 'zero-sum game' for the buyers and sellers and a margin business for the market maker, just as betting on horses is a zero-sum game for the gamblers as a whole.

Can you give me a practical example of real assets versus financial assets?

A financial asset is a legal contract to deliver a certain amount of money on certain conditions. A real asset is any other sort of asset – like land and buildings, or intellectual property, or trained employees.

A good way of explaining the distinction is to look at a set of company accounts. The assets in accounts are all either 'real' things or things which are defined purely in terms of amounts of money.

The assets which are defined as amounts of money are things like:

- trade debtors, also known as receivables, which is money due for product sold, or

- prepayments, which for accounting purposes can be thought of as the 'top and tail' ends of contracts which have 'money's worth' even if they are not cashable, or

- bank deposits, which are just contracts made by
banks promising to deliver cash on demand.

Trade creditors, accruals and bank overdrafts are the negatives of trade debtors, prepayments and bank deposits and are financial liabilities.

A company's accounts may also show 'real' assets – such as land, buildings, plant, machinery, know-how and intellectual property.

That all sounds quite neat. But what about goodwill? Or expenditure capitalised for exploring for oil? Are these real assets or financial assets?

A good question! They are 'real' assets. Capitalised exploration spend represents the cost of holes in the ground, maps and conceptual models. Goodwill represents the historic price paid for a business over and above its net asset value. The exploration and the business acquired are both 'real' things. The value is expressed in money terms. But the asset is not a contract for delivery of a specific amount of money in the future.

This sort of asset illustrates the ambivalence of the word 'real'. Real assets are 'real' in the sense of being things other than money. But that does not mean they have to be physical, tangible or visible.

Nor does it mean that they are easy to value. Real assets can be very difficult to value. Accounting gets around the difficulty of valuing real assets in two ways. It applies the tests for an 'accounting asset', which exclude many 'real' assets from the books. It also adopts the simplifying 'historical' cost convention which says that a real asset is worth what was paid for it – until such time as it becomes apparent that it is not!

Real assets don't sound so 'real'!

The adjective 'real' can conjure up a picture of solid, safe-as-houses, soundness. The aspect of a real asset which is very 'real' is its 'realness', not its financial value.

A sales force is a very 'real' asset. Although it exists at the balance sheet date, its value derives from the sales contracts it will sign up in the *future*. So it does not meet the test of an accounting asset.

A mine is a very real 'hole in the ground' – often of gigantic proportions. But its value is uncertain. The accounting value of the mine may be the cost of digging the hole. Whether or not that cost is 'recoverable' from future cash surpluses will only be known with certainty in the future.

Intellectual property is very 'real', but its financial value may vary enormously. It might be negative because money must be spent to maintain it. It might be positive because it represents a growing royalty stream.

And financial assets don't sound so real either!

It is all rather paradoxical. A loan is very real and durable. People who make the mistake of thinking that a loan is in some sense unreal learn otherwise if they fail to make repayments. A loan is not cancelled or extinguished unless the borrower declares bankruptcy or makes an 'accommodation' with his creditors. There are businesses which make a return by buying bad debts. These debts may be ten or more years old and the borrowers may have forgotten about them. But they still have a value. Debt collection businesses buy bad debts for a fraction of face value and then go after the borrowers to recover the loan.

On the other hand, when the government or the commercial banks cannot repay their loans or finance their losses, there is a risk that the whole system collapses – and that the value of many financial assets 'vanishes', turns into pumpkins and mice like Cinderella's coach and horses.

So how do I make a return out of owning a real asset?

As a generalisation, real assets do not 'spontaneously' produce a financial return. You can buy a field or a lorry. But unless you farm the field or use the lorry in some commercial venture these assets make no return. A real asset usually has to be put into some sort of business model and managed to make a return.

How is that different from the return from a financial asset?

A financial asset produces a rate of return in accordance with the terms of the contract which created it. So a bond is a contract to pay interest at a given rate and to return the initial capital on a given day. A trade credit is a contract to settle a debt in cash – without interest penalty if paid within the payment terms. An equity share is *sui generis,* a case apart. It is a contract in which shareholders have ownership rights to whatever surplus a business generates, but can only receive a cash share of those surpluses (dividends) as and when the board of directors directs.

The thing about financial assets (apart from equity) is that they produce a return which one can think of as 'spontaneous'. The return accrues *pro rata temporis* or proportional to the elapse of time. So a bond may accrue interest daily, based on an annual rate of interest. The owner does not have to 'work' the financial asset to get it to make a return in the same way that a manager of a printing business must work his printing presses to earn a return. The return on a financial asset is contractually due. The 'spontaneous' nature of returns on financial assets was a problem for early socialists – who thought that the returns were unjust or unfairly distributed across society. Of course, financial assets also require management and that entails work. Financial assets are managed in 'finance business models' and the work is no less important or necessarily less hard than that involved in other business models. Now that financial assets are almost universally owned in that everyone has a bank account and most people have some form of pension, any inequity is less of an issue.

Okay – you've explained how returns on financial assets differ from returns on real assets. Can you get back to the question – which is, where do we get the best returns?

To answer that question we have to elaborate on the inter-relationship of financial and real assets. And then we have to qualify returns with risk.

So how are financial and real returns related?

They are sort of the opposite sides of the same coin! Financial returns all ultimately derive from real assets, although the chain which links the two can be very long. But the real assets are only mobilised in the economic system because money – or money's worth – has been spent on them.

Let's look at a real business model to illustrate this. Take a well-known business model – an airline. All the returns – the cash surpluses generated by the airline project(s) – are made by real assets, the planes and the staff which transport the customers and their goods. If the business was directly owned by one person or by a group of people, the owners would receive any return made from operating the real assets, the planes.

Most airlines are incorporated so that the real assets are all owned by a company. The company raises capital by issuing shares and bonds. This capital is a liability of the company and a financial asset for the owners.

You can invest in the company's bonds and/or its shares. Both are financial assets for the investors and both are technically financial liabilities for the company. But equity shares are a paradoxical liability – a liability in name only.

This is a bit confusing. You are saying that equity shares are financial assets in name only then. Equity shares are really real assets?

Of course, in a technical sense an equity is a financial asset in as much as it is a legal claim which is defined in large part in terms of money. But I am saying that equities have more of the properties of real assets than they have of typical financial assets.

How are equities more like real assets than financial assets?

In a number of respects. First of all, financial assets except equity are somebody else's financial liability. So, for example, cash in the form of notes and coins is an asset in our hands but it is a liability of the central bank. A deposit with XYZ Bank is an asset for the depositor but a liability for the bank – a liability to deliver notes and coins if required.

Equity is different. When you own an equity share, no one has a liability to deliver cash to you against your share certificate. To all intents and purposes, you own a real asset. It is a more complicated real asset than the house you may own and live in. An equity share is an ownership interest in a collection of real assets combined and operated in some form of business model.

Secondly, just like a real asset, an equity share does not produce a financial return 'spontaneously', *pro rata temporis*. An equity share shares in the benefits, if any, of owning a business. The business must have a management team to operate the assets to get them to earn a return.

Thirdly, equities, like real assets, can be much more difficult to value than financial assets. A bond is worth face value at redemption because it is a contract to deliver a fixed sum of money on a fixed date. Between issue and redemption a fixed rate bond may change in value as interest rates vary, but at redemption the issuer will only pay back the face value. A floating rate bond is always worth face value unless there is some likelihood of default.

A real asset has a much wider range of possible values. Land may have different values depending on the use it is put to. Land used as a shopping centre is more valuable than land used to grow crops.

Equity has a very wide range of potential values. Its return is linked to the return on the underlying real asset, which may be volatile. If the equity is levered the equity becomes an option on the residual income after the prior claims of the debt have been met.

So what is the relationship of 'real' to financial assets?

Complex and ever-changing!

So how do equities and bonds differ in their relationship with real assets?

It is an interesting and important distinction. Both equities and bonds are technically financial assets rather than real assets. Ultimately all financial assets and liabilities are derivatives of 'real assets'. So the owners of financial assets can in theory look 'through' the financial asset that they own to see what real assets support the economic value of their financial asset.

The difference of the relationship of bonds and equity to the underlying real assets is one of *priority*. The bonds have prior rights to the returns from the real assets, but do not own the real assets. Bonds are usually backed by the credit of the whole company. This means that the equity stands as a buffer between the bondholders and the real assets.

When a company issues a bond it contracts to repay capital with interest. The backing for the promise may be the entire credit of the company or it may be specific hypothecated assets of the company.

Bond holders extract 'covenants' from the company. Under these covenants, the company promises to maintain minimum levels of assets and gross cashflow in relation to the value of the bonds. Provided the assets and cashflows of the business provide a big enough margin of safety over and above the interest and capital which is due, the bond holder does not overly worry if the bond is issued by a natural resources business or a capital goods business.

An equity share owns the real assets with no buffer at all. So, equity shareholders must be deeply concerned about the business model in which they own a share, because it is the residual profits of that model that will provide their return.

If the business has no borrowings, in other words is 'un-levered' or 'un-geared', then on a look-through basis the equity is entirely backed by real assets.

So equity shares are riskier than bonds?

Yes, more risky in a number of respects. The underlying assets and the business model which exploits them will have different intrinsic risks. The risks of banking are different from the risks of mining, for example. Then, on top of that, the corporate entity which owns the business projects will have a financial structure which may be more or less risky. So a business may be financed entirely with equity – in which case its capital structure is relatively less risky. Or the capital structure may include a large proportion of debt, in which case it may be very risky.

Bonds are relatively uniform in character. Equities, although they all have similar legal rights, derive their returns from different business models and capital structures. At one extreme, one equity share in a mature business with competitive advantages and a conservative capital structure may be less risky than most bonds. At another extreme, a bond issued by a company with very high borrowings and a cyclical business might be almost as risky as the pure equity claims on the company.

Equities sound much more complicated.

They are. The return on a bond is relatively easy to calculate because a bond is 'self-liquidating', which is to say that the issuer redeems it or buys the capital back for cash on a defined date. The return on an equity is much more difficult to compute because an equity share is irredeemable. Most companies do not have finite lives. And the managements of companies usually rather enjoy running them and so have an incentive to find new projects to replace old projects. Sometimes the 'corporate imperative' is to build a bigger business for management to manage, rather than to make a high rate of return.

Since an equity share does not self-liquidate, the only way to crystallise a cash value for it is to sell it on a market. As soon as a market is required to liquidate an asset, an element of subjectivity is introduced. The thing is worth what someone will pay for it – quite apart from its theoretical value, which is the present value of its estimated future cash surpluses.

You've talked about assets. You've distinguished economic and accounting assets from natural and social assets.
You've contra-distinguished assets defined in terms of money – financial assets – with real stuff that pre-exists money.
You've defined money. You've described money and financial assets as deriving from or as being derivatives of real stuff.

I think I understand what you are on about. But somehow I'm not quite satisfied with the answers. Can you tie these loose ends together for me?

Hmmm. I suppose I have sort of answered a whole lot of 'how' questions. Maybe you are groping for the answer to a 'why' question? *How* questions often have satisfactory answers. *Why* questions ultimately end up in mystery. The ultimate *why* question, why are we here?, is a question everyone must answer for themselves by consciously or unconsciously making choices.

No, I am just asking a 'how' question! How do these elements, money, financial assets and real assets, 'integrate' to build the economic system?

The answer to that can be summed up in an expression with rather a lot of syllables which means little to most people: maturity transformation. I described all of investment as an attempt to defeat the forces of time and said that investment builds civilisation. Well, both civilisation and investment are concerned about futurity and posterity. Without some interest in the future and future generations, some people lose any sense of responsibility. Some people pursue pleasure, hedonism. Some pleasures are fairly harmless. Dr Johnson said that if he had no cares for posterity he would spend his life chasing after pretty women in a horse-drawn carriage. Unfortunately some people take pleasure in unpleasant activities.

So how is maturity transformation at the heart of investment and civilisation?

Finance businesses take short-duration financial assets and transform them into longer-duration financial assets. Non-financial businesses take short-duration real assets and transform them into longer-term capabilities and capital goods. Financial and non-financial businesses do this within the framework of a civilisation which is consciously or unconsciously building a future.

Credit or belief in the future is at the heart of the financial system. Governments and central banks take a real asset, the industry and ingenuity of their citizens and tax payers, and transform it into long-term stocks of assets – real and financial capital. This capital takes many forms: stocks of trained people with stocks of knowledge; stocks of real capital like bridges and roads, and stocks of gold at the central bank to back paper money. Central banks take real long-term capital – gold reserves and governments' power to collect taxes – and transform it into a short-term financial asset, cash. The commercial banks take this short-term financial asset, cash, and turn it into longer-term financial assets, loans to customers. One might say that credit is to the economic ecosystem what water is the natural ecosystem.

Can you illustrate how banks transform maturities?

Yes, I can do it literally with a picture to represent the banking system's assets and liabilities. Here it is:

Bank balance sheet

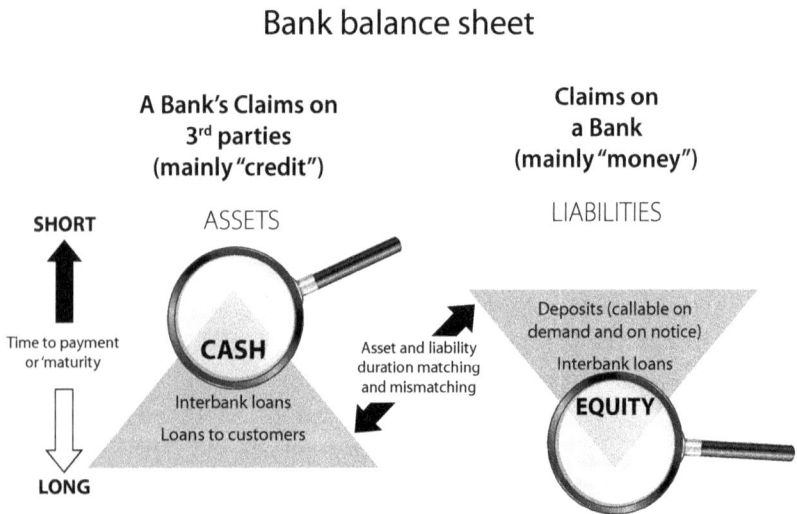

The diagram represents the assets and liabilities of a bank – which is a microcosm of the consolidated assets and liabilities of the banking system as a whole. You can see that banks hold relatively small (tiny) amounts of cash in relation to their loans or total assets and that they hold relatively large amounts of deposits in relation to their permanent capital – largely equity. The alchemy which the banking system performs to 'transform maturities' is to take deposits which are theoretically repayable on demand (or relatively short notice) and to use them to finance loans which may not be repayable for many years.

The balance sheets of capital intensive non financial corporations have a similar structure to a bank. So the electricity generation and distribution industry has a consolidated balance sheet in which cash is a relatively tiny part of fixed assets and total assets and equity is a relatively small part of total liabilities.

The difference between the balance sheets of banks and non financial corporations is that banks operate on much thinner margins and the leverage in their balance sheets is much, much, much larger.

The whole alchemy of maturity transformation depends on credit – faith in the future- with all the attendant paraphernalia of modern civilisation such as the rule of law, honest accounting, functioning markets and so on.

Is civilisation and investment succeeding?

Now that's a big question! Some spectacular falls or 'own goals' have been scored along the way: for example two world wars in Europe, Stalin's race to industrialise the Russian Empire and Mao's determination to modernise China, all of which cost millions of lives. A few own goals in an imperfect world are inevitable. Unfortunately in some parts of the world some governments seem to specialise in own goals.

Aren't things worse now than for some time?

Some things are different this time. For a start there are more people alive than at any previous time in history. In 1920 there were 'only' two billion people on the planet. Now there are seven billion.

To get an historical perspective everyone should read Carlo Cippola's *The Economic History of World Population* first published nearly 50 years ago.[12]

The additional billions naturally wish to have the advantages of technological progress and to enjoy many things we take for granted in our civilisation such as electricity. This puts a strain on resources and the natural ecosystem.

What else is different?

We have just lived through the largest credit expansion in history.

It is difficult to get a sense of the proportions of this. Very large numbers are mentioned in the media. But properly consolidated figures are seldom presented.

One way of getting some perspective on the way debt has grown in the last fifteen years is to use figures prepared for the National Accounts. Debt as a proportion of total assets in the UK National Accounts grew rapidly. The picture looks like this:[13]

---

[12] Carlo Cipolla: *The Economic History of World Population*, 1962.

[13] Source UK National Accounts 2011 Edition, Total financial assets have been adjusted for equity holdings and life insurance technical reserves and divided by two to compensate for double counting.

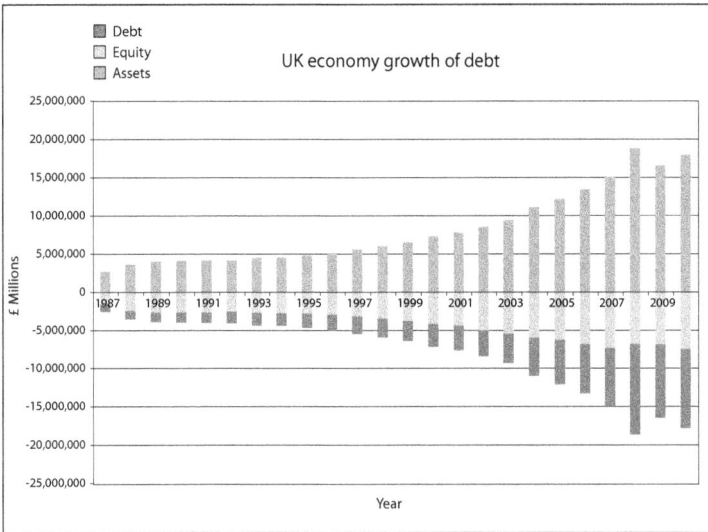

UK economy growth of debt

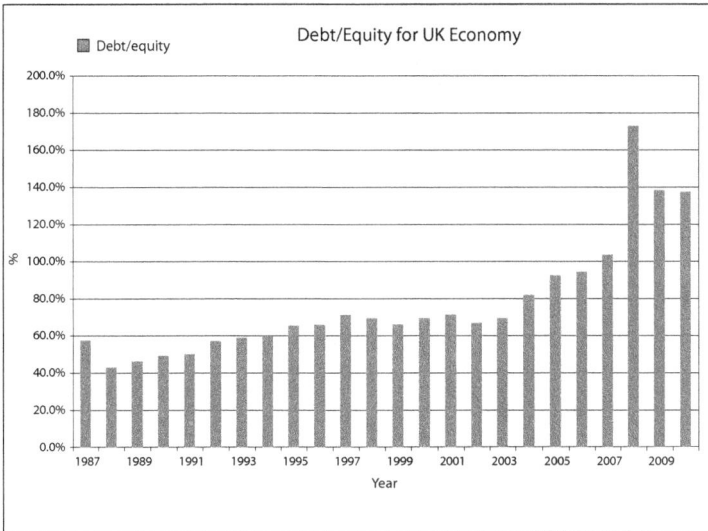

Debt/Equity for UK Economy

Debt has grown on a similar trajectory in the USA over the same period – and in many other countries.

How important are these two factors?

If we look back over history there were hundreds of years in which per capita incomes for most people did not change at all. By contrast, in the last two hundred years there has been pretty consistent growth in per capita incomes in 'western' civilisation. Given that the population grew significantly over this period the rise in incomes per capita has been especially remarkable.

Of the many factors which have made this possible, growth in the per capita consumption of energy and growth in per capita financial credit are particularly important. Per capita energy consumption has grown because of the availability of cheap fossil fuels, which in turn has been part of the reason for the growth in the availability of credit. If these long-term trends are coming to an end, future civilisation will have to be different.

Significant and irreversible damage to the natural ecosystem means that the amount of 'natural capital' available to future generations is smaller than before. One variable which might compensate is that the stock of intellectual capital or knowledge is greater.

Will the knowledge be used wisely?

Civilisation is a fragile construct and needs nurture. As world population increases and cheap energy resources become scarcer, more strain will be placed on the natural and economic ecosystems.

Electorates are sold two economic paradigms: 'free market' systems and centrally planned systems. Neither is perfect. The collapse of most centrally planned systems and their association with political oppression has discredited most extreme forms of central planning. One of the attractions of market systems is that they are democratic in the sense that every dollar or euro or pound spent in a market expresses the implicit opinion of a buyer and seller. Markets are a critical component of maturity transformation. But markets for longer duration real and financial assets can be very fragile. Liquidity and volume in these markets can come by fits and starts and at times can completely 'evaporate'. Market 'fundamentalists', as George Soros describes them, tend to the view that markets are self-organising and can be relied upon to achieve socially and economically acceptable if not optimal solutions. Real world experience of markets diminishes such unrealistic expectations. Many markets develop spontaneously but most are consciously created and they all need to be regulated and self-regulated to prosper.

Is economics enough?

As Ernst Schumacher said, economics is the modern rule book or religion. It is the non-denominational religion to which most governments subscribe. The moral legitimacy of economics is based upon acceptance of the 'fairness' of prices and the belief that, on the whole, free market systems create prices which produce socially acceptable outcomes. The weakness of economics is that prices do not and cannot perfectly capture value. Economic value is a narrow thing: value to an investor on a timescale which, on an historical scale, is very short. Economics calls the indirect consequences of economic activity 'externalities' and has difficulty pricing them. For most of history economics has treated natural resources as 'free'. Economics struggles to value existence and its essential mystery, also known as Nature or God.

How do markets transform maturities?

Everyone uses and benefits from assets which outlast their own lives. Hundreds of man years have been invested in many of the gadgets we use every day. We cannot replicate the investment ourselves. It is markets and trade which bring us the benefits of other people's investment. In Newton's analogy, it is markets which allow us 'to stand on the shoulders of giants'.

If each person had to be self-sufficient no one would have time to do more than forage for food.

The lives or durations of some real and financial assets are very long. A government bond may be irredeemable, meaning that the government has no obligation to repay the loan. An infrastructure asset like a port or a railway might have a life of a hundred or more years. A limited liability company has an indefinite life.

Long duration assets are difficult to create, manage and price. Markets alleviate some of the problems. Most people would not buy an asset which they could not directly use themselves if they could not sell it for any value until 30 years had elapsed. Markets create the possibility that the 'torch of ownership' can be passed from one cohort of investors to another as the asset moves through time.

Markets, time and money

It looks as if markets are essential to equity investment?

Since a corporation has an indefinite life, an equity share is not 'self-liquidating'. So the main way and sometimes the only way to get a cash return on an equity share is to sell it to someone else on a market. So yes, markets are more essential to equity investment than to investing in bonds.

Markets perform some cunning tricks. They convert multi-form stuff into 'uni-form' stuff; that is, money. They put prices on things which in some respects are priceless. They create liquidity in assets that are not intrinsically very liquid.

How do markets create liquidity?

Markets do lots of things that are hard to replicate. They enable aggregation and disaggregation of quantities. Large quantities can be built up and dissipated in a market by bringing many participants together. Markets allow the participants to express their opinions about the future in the prices of the real and financial assets. They also enable 'maturity mismatching'. Long-term assets, 30-year bonds or nuclear generation businesses can be traded by economic units which have neither the intention nor the balance sheets to hold the assets to maturity.

Are markets efficient?

There is long-standing tension between 'planned' solutions and 'free market' solutions. The extreme paradigms of 'free markets' and central planning are mythological creatures. In practice, what exists in most places is regulated markets.

A definition of a perfectly efficient market might be where value and price are identical all the time. Perfect efficiency of this sort is impossible because the future cannot be predicted with sufficient accuracy. The reason price and value diverge is uncertainty about the future.

Academic studies seek to test the 'efficiency' of markets. What these show is that there are no simple trading rules which will show consistently better than average results. In other words, they show that markets are generally efficient in the sense that when properly regulated, they do not have systemic biases which can be easily exploited to make money. That is not really a very surprising discovery. Like bookmakers, markets price the odds so that it is difficult to make easy money out of them.

What happens if there are no banks and no markets?

A world without banks or markets would be rather rigid and inflexible.

In general, economic units would have to keep the real and financial assets which they own all the way through to maturity.

Maturity in the case of a bond is the final repayment date, and in the case of a real asset like a car, it is the time when it has worn out or is no longer worth repairing. Economic units would have to match the maturity of their assets and liabilities more carefully – because it would be more difficult to change their minds by either selling in a market or by going to a bank and borrowing against the assets.

Why would that be?

Suppose that you had some savings and that you wanted to make an investment. Over what timescale should you seek to tie up your capital? Your choice of two years or ten years or any other period may be more or less arbitrary. Even if you expect to retire in ten years, you still have a choice of the length of time for which you wish to tie up your money.

If you bought a financial asset, you would be able to know for how long you had tied up your money. So, if you bought a five-year bond you would know that the bond would liquidate back into cash in five years' time, and you would know what nominal rate of interest it would pay you in the interval.

If you bought a real asset you might have a fair idea of its life and its rate of return. But it would be a good deal more uncertain. Suppose, for the sake of argument, you found a real asset with a five-year life in which you could invest. It might be a 'white van man' project. The main asset in this case would be the 'white van' itself. Its life might be roughly five years and you might either operate the real asset yourself, or you might employ someone to do it for you, or you might supply the capital to buy the van to an entrepreneur to operate.

If there were no banks and no markets you would have to own the financial asset you had invested in – the five-year bond – or the real asset – the white van man project – to maturity before you could recover your capital. Five years is not long to wait.

But if the project was a new oil basin or a new power station, the horizon might be 30 years. Imagine not being able to trade such an asset for 30 years.

It looks as if it is much easier to buy a bond than it is to buy into a business.

Yes, a bond is a much simpler thing to evaluate than a business. A bond ought to be less risky. And the returns from a bond ought most of the time to be lower than the returns on the business. After all, if the returns on the bond were much higher than the return on the business, the owner of the business would not find it profitable to borrow.

But what has this got to do with time?

Time comes into it because it is not just a choice between buying a bond or a business. It is a choice of how long one wants to be invested for. Bonds come in different maturities. And businesses also have different maturities.

What do you mean by different 'maturities'?

The maturity of a bond is the date when it 'matures'! That is to say, the day on which it pays back its face value. Investors put down cash to buy a bond. In return they get a stream of future cash payments culminating in the final 'redemption' of the bond. A bond might have a 5% coupon, or interest rate, and a repayment date in year ten. This means that the investor will get an interest payment, or coupon, of 5% each year and that the face value of the bond, normally 100, will pay back in year ten. The maturity of a ten-year bond is ten years.

A more precise measure of 'maturity' is 'duration'. Duration is the weighted average of the present values of each of the cash payments. Since the final bullet repayment of 100 in year 10 is orders of magnitude greater than the annual coupons, the duration of a 10-year bond is close to its maturity, 10, if interest rates are low.[14]

The maturity date of a business is much more subjective than for a bond, but is nonetheless quite real. A business is just a project or a collection of projects. A business project has a finite life unless it is extended or adapted by further investment. The corporations which own the business projects typically have unlimited lives. They continue to exist until they are deliberately wound up or they go bust. If we look through the corporate owner to the underlying business project, the 'life' and renewal cycle of the projects can be estimated.

Can you give me some examples of business projects with different lives?

For some businesses, determining the life of the key project is quite easy. A mining project will typically have disclosed figures for ore reserves and resources. The mine plan will set out how many years it will take to exhaust existing proven reserves. To continue the business beyond the life of existing reserves, a new project must be created by proving further reserves.

Something similar happens in the oil business. Each oil field is a finite resource.

In capital goods business models the key products need to be periodically 'refreshed' or redesigned. This requires new investment. Conceptually each product iteration can be thought of as a new project.

In service business models the capital equipment used to provide the service needs to be periodically renewed – be it aeroplanes or power stations or hotels or human capital. If an airline owns

---

[14] The duration of a 10-year bond with a 5% coupon discounted at 5% pa is 8.1 years. The same bond with a 1% coupon has a duration of 9.57 years. The duration of a zero coupon bond coincides with its maturity.

all its own planes, then the remaining life of its business project could be thought of as the average unexpired life of its planes. If the airline leased all its planes the remaining life of the project would be the unexpired portion of the leases.

The duration of business projects can be looked at in terms of the duration of the typical project and in terms of how often the project can be renewed. The fact that the project has a short life does not mean that the business has a short life. Some process and distribution models have relatively short project lives – but the projects renew almost indefinitely.

And the fact that the project has a very long life – such as a tunnel or a railway – does not mean that the business itself will have an equally long life. Competition, substitutes and solvency may all cut short the economic life of the business before the life of its core asset or project has expired.

How useful is it to know the duration of the cash surpluses of a project?

Having a rough idea of the duration of a project is not of academic interest only. It can give useful insights into their risks.

Short duration projects by definition get recycled and re-priced more often. As a result, their industries may be more competitive. But they tend to be less risky. Supply of capacity in industries with shorter duration projects tends to adjust more quickly than in industries with very long duration projects.

The duration of the project cashflows also affects how easy it may be to finance the project – the financing risk. Short duration projects are typically easier to finance. Long duration projects need a larger proportion of long maturity finance, and the short maturity finance needs to be periodically refinanced.

**Aren't there several different durations involved?
Doesn't the duration of our investment differ from the
duration of the business?**

The duration we choose for our own investment will almost
certainly be shorter than that of most business corporations,
since corporations have indefinite lives.

We have to separate out several elements: the corporation,
the projects owned and operated by the corporation, and our
investment.

At the corporate level different strategies can have dramatic
effects on duration. The board might decide to sell off business
units or return cash to shareholders, for example.

At the project level duration varies over the life of a project. At
the start of a new project, cashflows tend to be negative and
duration is long and uncertain. Toward the end of a project,
cashflows tend to be positive and duration is short.

Since most investors are not 'buying for keeps', the duration
of the cashflows that they receive depends on the availability
of a liquid market in which they can sell their shares. One
way of thinking about the *expected* duration of shareholder
cashflows is that it increases with the price of the shares. Unless
the expected cash surpluses generated by the projects and the
dividends generated by the corporations both increase, a higher
share price implies a longer duration and therefore higher risk.

Mismatching the duration of the cashflows of assets and
liabilities involves risk.

**What do you mean by mismatching durations on assets
and liabilities?**

Suppose that there's no market for 'second-hand' investments.
Suppose a project has a life of five years, say. If we invest in a

five-year project at its start, we will not know for certain what its average annual return is until the end of the five years. Unless there is a market for shares in the project, we will not get our money out again until year five.

So we have to match our time horizon to the 'life' of the investment?

It can create a serious problem if the time horizons are not matched, especially if the investment is not marketable or quoted. If you had a liability that you knew you had to pay in year five, school fees or the balance of a mortgage loan perhaps, you would want an asset to be available to pay the liability. If the asset had not matured by the time you needed the money, at best you are inconvenienced and at the very worst you are bust.

Does it matter if the investment is a bond, a share or a house if the time horizons are matched?

The problem is that unless the investment is a bond, you cannot know its duration with certainty or near certainty. One of the key differences between 'real' and financial assets is the ease with which their respective durations can be estimated. The duration of the cashflows from financial assets like bonds can be accurately estimated. By contrast, the duration of cash surpluses from real assets like shares and houses is very uncertain.

Real assets suffer from duration risk and from liquidity risk. The duration of the cashflows of an equity share or a house is uncertain and, partly as a result, the liquidity and price of these real assets is also uncertain. Although the long-term returns from real assets ought to be higher than the returns on financial assets, they are less 'bankable'.

Bankability, or acceptability of an asset to a bank, is related to certainty of liquidity as well as of money value. Managing duration mismatches is at the heart of what a bank does. Assets of uncertain duration are less 'bankable' even if they deliver higher returns, because they may bring unacceptable risk.

Do returns correlate with duration?

In a crude and very general sense they do. Short duration assets make smaller returns than longer duration assets. This is quite intuitive.

An asset with a duration of three months is not likely to give a return of hundreds of per cent. There are very few projects that liquidate in three months which can produce that sort of return. A typical three-month duration project might be to finance a 'trade receivable' – in other words, to give a supplier the working capital to build goods ordered by a buyer. The supplier can pay us for the working capital received and can repay us when he receives payment from the buyer – in, say, 90 or 120 days. This sort of project is short duration and relatively low risk. You can see that the amount the seller and the buyer can afford to pay for the money is limited.

A long duration asset can produce higher returns. The longer time period allows time for a project to replicate itself. A project to build a mobile phone creates some core technologies and some specific phones. The life of the particular phone model might be very short, one to three years. But the core technology can be renewed and re-used in future phone models. The returns on the core technology tend to multiply over time as it is leveraged over a broader product range and a larger installed base of customers.

But can't we buy and sell all these investments in the market? How does this affect their duration?

The discussion so far has assumed that there is *no* market, that we are buying directly into the assets, into the projects themselves.

If one invests directly in the assets or project and buys the shares 'for keeps', the return will depend on the dividends which the company pays out, which in turn will depend on the returns on the projects which the company undertakes.

In the absence of markets, investments in these sorts of projects are not liquid and offer few opportunities for second thoughts or changing one's mind. The investments made by government and government agencies tend to be of this sort – investments for keeps where the duration of the investment depends on a project life cycle.

So what conclusion have we reached on the duration issue?

Well, we can make some straightforward generalisations.

Only invest in unquoted businesses/securities if their cashflows match your own time horizon. It is probably wisest only to invest in unquoted businesses if one has a degree of control.

So, if you have a one-year horizon it is probably best to buy a one-year duration asset – like a short-term bond. If you buy a long duration asset like an equity and expect to be able to sell it in one year at a profit, you may be disappointed.

Only invest in quoted securities/business if you have an opinion on the cashflows of the underlying assets. Investing can imply being short as well as long.

Quoted and unquoted shares

What happens when there is a market for the investment?

The existence of a market for second-hand shares makes a huge difference. If one thinks of the underlying investment as 'reality', one can think of the market in shares in the underlying investment as creating a model of reality – a meta reality, if you like. The underlying assets generate the cashflows; the market generates an implicit opinion of what those cashflows are worth today. One of the interesting features of a market is that cause and effect runs from reality to meta reality, but also from market opinion to cash reality. If you think about it, it is hard to argue that the meta reality is any less 'real' than the thing we labelled 'reality'. Money itself is, after all, a meta reality.

Give me an example of that.

Okay. Suppose we have a business with one project which renews every five years. The underlying duration of the project is five years. The underlying duration of the business may be ten years, depending on how many iterations the project will go through.

Someone might buy up shares in the market and make a cash takeover offer for the business because he wants to get control of the project. He might want to accelerate replication of the project. Or, he might want to close down the project at the end of its life and re-deploy the capital. Either way, the takeover offer has changed the duration of the shares in the business. A five- or ten-year duration asset has become a ninety-day duration asset. The takeover bid is an example of market opinion changing the underlying reality.

Should we prefer to invest in shares quoted on the market or directly into an unquoted business?

As a generalisation, we should prefer to invest in the market; that is, in the quoted shares rather than directly in the underlying business.

The main reason is that having a market for opinion in the value of a share creates additional degrees of freedom. It creates the opportunity to arbitrage opinions rather than only to select the best projects and invest in them directly.

Investing directly in an unquoted business is difficult for private investors because:

- The minimum quantum of investment is large.

- Unquoted investments are illiquid. Exit date is uncertain.

- Unless a significant proportion of the business is owned, there are opportunities for the management/majority to oppress the minority; for example, buy them out at an undervalue.

- The standard and regularity of information may be worse than in quoted shares.

Explain more about the additional degrees of freedom that investing in quoted shares creates.

Okay. A quoted share expresses an opinion about the value of the underlying projects. If you disagree with this opinion you can buy or sell the shares.

You can do things in the market which are impossible in the real world project:

- You can open and close your exposure to the underlying project with a buy or a sell. As a result you do not have to match precisely your cashflow horizon with the cashflows of the project. The 'buy-for-keeps' investor in an unquoted project has to wait for the project to self-liquidate – which might take decades.

- You can also buy and sell the shares in the 'wrong' order. In other words, you can sell the shares first and hope to buy them back cheaper if you think that the market opinion on the project is too optimistic.

Buying and selling in the market allows one to take a view of both the underlying project and of other people's opinion of it. In other words, it allows one to exploit or to be a victim of other people's overreactions, hysteria, euphoria, folly and misperceptions.

Are you saying that the lack of regular pricing makes unquoted shares riskier?

Well, an investment in an unquoted company may not give an opportunity for the price to be re-visited after the investment has been made, if the assumptions upon which the price was based turn out to have been wrong. Investments in immature projects are seldom 'one shot', one-round investments. They require several subsequent investment rounds. So investment agreements for unquoted investments often have so-called 'downround' clauses. These allow the shares of the first-round investors to be re-priced to the level of any lower price used in any subsequent fund raising.

What makes one price a better price than another price for the opportunity to own any particular set of potential cashflows?

The thing that makes the difference is the distance of the price from the value.

What the value may be is to some extent a matter of individual judgement. There is not just one value for a business. The value you receive lies in the future in some mix of future cash receipts and/or resale value. The price paid for the business and its projects implies a stream of future cash surpluses. There is not just one stream of cashflows that justifies the price paid. Many different streams of cash surpluses with different amounts and timings may have the same present value. And, of course, there are other streams of cashflows that justify higher and lower prices.

Many different combinations of cashflows may have the same present value. What makes some combinations more attractive is their relative riskiness. Riskiness encompasses many different things. The further out in the future the cash surpluses lie, the riskier they tend to be. Whether the expected cash surpluses will in fact materialise depends on the business model, the management and its strategy, and the credit cycle, and may depend on whether the company can raise new capital.

The existence of a market for the shares creates an interesting duality. On the one hand, there is the underlying business/ project with its cashflows, and on the other hand, there is the market perception of the present value of the 'whole of life' cashflows of the project.

Not all markets are 'equal' in terms of their depth and liquidity. And the nature of the market for a share tends to change as the projects which the share participates in mature. If there is a liquid market in the shares, it provides a daily, 'real-time' mechanism in which the assumptions underlying the future value can be re-priced.

So why would one ever invest directly in an underlying project?

It really comes down to valuation and to control. Unquoted investments usually command lower prices. This is partly because they have the disadvantages mentioned – illiquidity, and hence fewer degrees of freedom. Even so, if the underlying project is sufficiently interesting and comes at a sufficiently discounted price, unquoted investments can be very attractive.

What happens if the market closes?

It depends how far apart price and value may be or, to put it another way, how far apart the market meta reality is from the underlying cashflow reality. If the two are close together then the closure of the market for a period is more of an inconvenience than a disaster. If the two are miles apart then market closure can cause massive disruption.

One can think of the market as a machine which permits durations to be mismatched. An investor in a power utility buys a concept of a stream of cashflows, which may stretch out for 50 years or more – most of which he will never partake in himself. The duration of a power station project cashflows might be 30 years. The investor might plan to hold the shares for the next five years. The dividends the company pays in the next five years are a tiny fraction of the total value of the business. The market allows successive 'cohorts' of investors to buy and hold the shares for durations which are individually much shorter than the duration of the project.

If the market closes, a whole lot of people who had short investment horizons suddenly become 'long-term investors'. The cynic's definition of a long-term investment is a 'short-term investment which went wrong'!

Without the market, people have to hold their investments to maturity. For long duration assets the constituency of people with long investment horizons may be reduced by closing the market. The returns on long duration assets would almost certainly have to rise.

Do markets ever close?

They do close from time to time. Sometimes there is a 'moment of truth' when the participants realise that the underlying reality and the meta reality are miles apart, and there is paralysis whilst the participants wait for new information and understanding. During this period, liquidity in the market can dry up completely – because no one is quite sure of what they are buying and selling.

Markets have also closed in time of war. The London Stock Exchange closed for several months at the start of WW1 and for short periods during WW2, but remarkably stayed open for most of WW2, although on much reduced activity. When almost the entire productive capacity of a country is devoted to producing materials for a war, it becomes a bit irrelevant what the market price for companies producing luxury handbags may be, and whether it stimulates additional investment in handbag production. The economy becomes a command economy. This is what happened in the economies of the countries involved in WW2.

Does this mean that the market is unnecessary?

There are many things that are not strictly necessary, but we should prefer not to be without. In one sense, the market is not necessary – in that, strictly speaking, society could get by without it. On the other hand, having a market has numerous benefits, which greatly outweigh the risks. The fact that the London Stock Exchange stayed open throughout most of both World Wars suggests that a minimum level of market activity is a necessity.

One benefit of the market is that it expresses opinion – in particular, opinion about prices and therefore about the future. If the price of electricity rises, it is an expression of opinion. People and businesses who bought electricity at higher prices took a view. That view might have been that more electricity will be demanded than is currently being or is expected to be supplied. Or it might be an opinion that supply is somehow constrained. The higher price ultimately stimulates investment in new capacity in the electricity supply chain – which ends up giving people what they want.

In a command economy all these micro decisions have to be made by a group of politicians, civil servants and generals. In time of national emergency, it is possible that they 'know best'.

But in time of peace, it is hard to believe that they could ever access and process all the information needed to make good decisions about all the micro variables that need to be priced.

Another benefit is that a market allows investors to invest in cash-flow streams which they will not personally live long enough to receive. It allows durations to be mismatched. This creates liquidity and flexibility and so reduces costs. If the only people who could invest in 30-year projects were institutions which could be sure they would be around for all of the 30 years, the pool of available capital would be smaller and its cost higher.

Taking a short position

You said that a market created the freedom to go short. That does not sound like an expression of confidence in the market.

Taking a short position is, paradoxically, an expression of confidence in the market – because the short sale is based on the belief that the market will be open, so that the trade can be closed by buying the shares back.

So how is going short investing?

Investing is about putting capital at risk and seeking to make a return on that capital. Investment is generally thought of as putting money into real, productive assets and getting the assets to make a return. Once you have a market, a meta reality, which expresses a view of the value of the assets and their returns, you have the ability to take a contrary view of the assets and the returns they will make. So you can 'invest' in the opinion that the assets will not make the returns that are implied by their price.

A long position assumes that there is sufficient demand for the product, that the assets will have a return in their current use and that the price is low or 'fair'. A short position assumes that demand for the product will be insufficient, that the returns from the assets will fall and that the price is too high. Long and short opinions are in theory not symmetrically opposite because the lowest a share price can fall is to is zero, whilst there is no theoretical limit on how high it can rise. But in practical terms, all businesses and projects have finite lives and values. All economic value is finite.

So why is 'shorting' controversial?

Some of the controversy is aroused by emotion. Nobody likes other people to 'rain on their parade'. A number of vested interests, like the management and its advisers, may have invested in a particular picture of reality. A short seller is perceived as a bit of an iconoclast – breaking the beautiful picture that has been created.

Some of the controversy is also aroused by potential market abuses. The market reality is supposed to reflect the underlying reality. But the market meta reality also affects reality – like the ability to raise new money in the market. Short sellers may change prices and perceptions to such an extent that management plans have to change. That may be a good thing. But it can be a bad thing.

Markets are not perfect and have to be managed. People can go long or short to manipulate a price. Regulation is in place to minimise manipulation.

CHAPTER 4

What rate of return can I get on financial assets?

Okay. So you have explained that we are interested in a particular sort of returns – economic returns – and that to get them we can buy 'real' or 'financial' assets. You've also explained that investment is about defeating the forces of time and that the returns we can expect on different assets varies with the 'duration' of the assets. I still want to pin you down on where I can get the best returns.

The holder of a pure financial asset like a bond (as opposed to an equity share or a financial derivative) knows what cashflows he is contractually entitled to receive. So he knows when he will be repaid and what his nominal rate of return will be. The real rate of return that he actually achieves will also depend on the rate of price inflation and the possibility of contractual default by the borrower.

There are huge, indeed colossal, quantities of financial assets in issue: government bonds, corporate bonds, municipal bonds and so on.[15] The markets for government bonds are usually deep and liquid, and so their prices are quite reliable. Some corporate bonds may only trade sporadically and markets for them can be characterised by 'evaporative' liquidity.

---

[15] The Securities Industry and Financial Markets Association (SIFMA) estimated that the total value of outstanding Outstanding Bond Market Debt as at 31 December 2006 was $27.4 trillion.

The prices of bonds of different maturities reveal the interest rate attributable to cash payments at different times in the future. These interest rates show the price of credit – money due for delivery at different dates in the future.

How do I get to see these prices of money for future delivery?

The easiest way to see the interest rate for money deliverable at a precise date in the future is to look at a 'zero coupon' bond. This is because this sort of bond only makes one cash payment. The amount of the cash repayment, the time period and the price paid for the bond allow the interest rate attributable to the payment date to be calculated.

Using bonds with a variety of different maturities and coupons, the prices of money for delivery at different dates in the future can be calculated with a bit of algebra. These can be plotted on a chart to show a 'yield curve'.

Can you give me an example?

Yes. Suppose you found a zero coupon bond repaying at 100 in 10 years' time and that the price today was 50. There is only one compound rate of interest that will grow 50 so that it is 100 in precisely 10 years. It happens to be 7.17%. If you found a zero coupon bond with a redemption date in 11 years' time, you would know the 'price' of 11-year credit. Suppose the 11-year bond cost 45, then the compound rate of interest is 7.5%. Given these 'dots on the line', it is not difficult arithmetically to fill in the spaces 'between the dots', so to speak. Bond traders arbitrage different prices along the yield curve – and profit by trading large volumes at small margins.

The chart below shows the actual Euro Zone yield curve on one date, 9 April 2009, as well as on all the days in the prior year for AAA-rated Euro Zone government bonds. The curve is created by using market prices and by interpolating the spaces between the dots to create a smooth line. The curve was calculated by the European Central Bank and was created on its website.

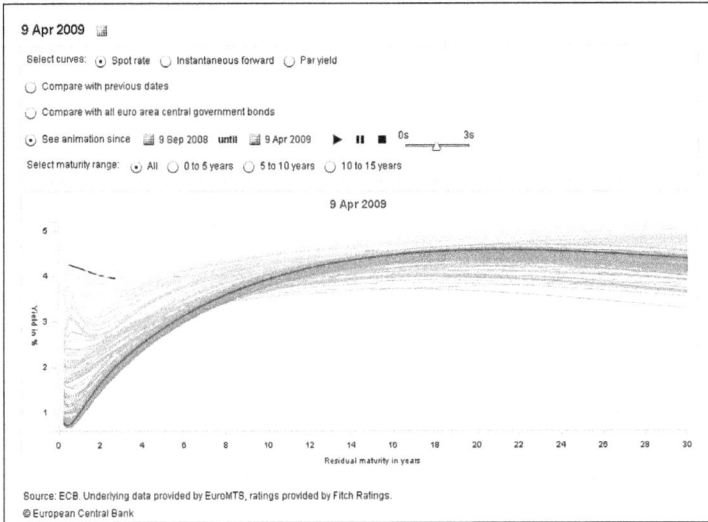

9 Apr 2009

Select curves: ⦿ Spot rate ◯ Instantaneous forward ◯ Par yield

◯ Compare with previous dates

◯ Compare with all euro area central government bonds

⦿ See animation since ▦ 9 Sep 2008 until ▦ 9 Apr 2009 ▶ ❚❚ ■ 0s ____ 3s

Select maturity range: ⦿ All ◯ 0 to 5 years ◯ 5 to 10 years ◯ 10 to 15 years

9 Apr 2009

Source: ECB. Underlying data provided by EuroMTS, ratings provided by Fitch Ratings.
© European Central Bank

What does this curve show us?

Most obviously, it shows us that the rate of return on government bonds varies with maturity. Long maturity bonds typically pay a higher nominal interest rate.

It also shows that the curve moves around quite a lot, particularly in periods of financial turmoil like the 2008/09 'Global Financial Crisis'.

If I want a high rate of interest, why would I not just buy a longer maturity bond?

You might well do just that – buy a ten-year bond. And after a few years you might trade it in and buy another bond with a remaining life of ten years.

The reason not to buy the ten-year bond, but to buy the one-year bond instead, is risk.

The longer maturities are riskier. The reason is that you are locking in a fixed rate of interest for a long time. Locking in an interest rate for a long time is riskier than locking it in for a short time. If interest rates were to change during the life of the long bond, this would affect more cashflows over a longer time period and so have a larger effect on the price/value of the bond than for a short bond. If you hold the long bond to maturity, that is until it is redeemed, you will not actually realise a cash loss because you did not sell. But if interest rates have risen over the whole of the life of the bond, perhaps because the rate of inflation has increased, the value you receive on redemption will represent a loss in 'real' terms, even if not in nominal terms.

Statistically, the way that risk is measured is as the variability of returns around an average, measured by 'standard deviation'. The prices of long-dated bonds are more variable than the prices of short-dated bonds. The cause of the variability of the capital value of the bond is the effect of locking down the interest rate. In general, the sensitivity of a bond to changes in interest rates increases with the duration of the bond.

This means that bonds are a way of expressing an opinion about interest rates. If you believed that interest rates were going to fall, you would buy a long bond. If you thought that interest rates were likely to rise, you would own short-dated bonds.

Most people have an intuitive sense of the rate of inflation and whether interest rates represent good value.

So, what determines the respective returns on short-term and long-term money?

Three things, I suppose: government policy, 'market forces' and inflation, which is both a cause and an effect of the first two factors.

Can you explain how government policy affects the returns or the 'price of money'?

Well, remember that cash is at root a government-'created' product. The central banks create cash and commercial banks 're-sell' it. It's a bit like a software company writing a suite of software programmes and 'Value Added Re-sellers' distributing the software.

Of course, the distributors add enormous value to the product. In some cases they adapt it beyond recognition. The product creator – a government or a Microsoft – does not have total control over what the distributors do with the product. Distributors can write their own software modules and sell consulting hours alongside the software, for example.

The 'distribution' of money and credit is more complex than the distribution of most products. Where money is concerned, the commercial banks use the product, cash, to create bank credit as well as bank deposits. The ratio of the banking sector's portfolio of loans and deposits to central bank cash is very large.

There are levers of control on the central and commercial banks. And ultimately, these levers are subject to political control. Many politicians disowned any responsibility for the Global Financial Crisis of 2008/09, claiming that the problem was 'global capitalism', not government regulation! Of course, the causes were systemic. But the banking industry is tightly regulated. It is illegal to operate a bank without a licence from the central bank. To get a licence, it is necessary to demonstrate that the company has sufficient capital and that 'fit and proper' people will manage it. The ultimate responsibility for the system rests with the ultimate 'owner' and regulator of the system – government and politicians.

Hmmm. So how does government set the price of money?

Let's be specific. The central bank has enormous power to set the price of very *short-term* money – cash and the price at which it lends to commercial banks. This is because it has considerable control of 'liquidity'. It can literally create cash and deliver it to the banking system.

Walter Bagehot, one of the first people to analyse the banking system, explained the mechanism in his 1873 book, *Lombard Street*. The central bank's power to affect very short-term interest rates is related to its power to create large amounts of cash in relation to the pre-existing stock of cash.

Central banks are not in such a powerful position to 'fix' longer term interest rates. This is because the markets for longer term bonds are very large and central banks are relatively small participants in them.

Doesn't the government intervene in the market?

Government creates the framework for the market, manages it and intervenes in it. It does this by setting the structure of the market – and managing it.

Government usually owns the central bank. The Bank of England, quaintly known as the Old Lady of Threadneedle Street, was unusual in that it was owned by a collection of 'merchant' banks until 1945, a kind of self-regulatory arrangement where it was the bankers' bank. When it was nationalised, Keynes quipped that the government had made an 'honest woman' of the bank. He meant that since the central bank was an instrument of government policy it might as well be owned by government. The independence of central banks subsequent to nationalisation is now a greater problem: governments are able to exercise their 'conjugal rights' and demand credit when they feel like it.

Government is a key player in the debt markets, supplying 'sovereign debt'. By issuing new bonds and redeeming old bonds, it manages the maturity of the stock of sovereign debt. It can also seek to influence the relative price of its bonds by buying and selling them in the market without redeeming them.

Government can also ask – or tell – the central bank to buy assets and create the money with which to buy the assets, a process known as Quantitative Easing (QE). QE involves expanding the balance sheet of the central bank by buying assets on the one hand and creating cash on the other. It is intended to inject cash into the economy. QE may be relatively conservative or reckless, depending on what assets the central bank buys. Central banks have a preference for highly liquid securities and hence are most likely to buy government bonds from the financial sector and the public. Buying existing or 'second-hand' government debt is not necessarily inflationary.

QE seldom involves buying new government bonds. Buying new government bonds would be more like 'printing money' for the government to spend. Of course buying second-hand bonds from existing holders who use the proceeds to buy new government bonds may have the effect of indirectly financing the government deficit. In practice buying second-hand government bonds is more subtle than buying new government bonds.

The central bank has the freedom to sell the bonds back to the market, the reverse of QE, known as Quantitative Tightening or QT. Alternatively, when the bonds purchased by the central bank mature they get redeemed and the original QE automatically reverses.

Through the central bank, the government regulates the entire banking system. The regulatory system works through three key levers: setting the amount of capital banks must hold – the 'capital to asset' ratio; setting (implicitly or explicitly) the amount of cash banks must hold – the cash to deposits ratio; and by setting short-term interest rates.

So what is the 'money supply' and does the government control it?

Ever since Croesus, king of Lydia in Asia Minor, modern Turkey, invented gold coinage, money has been associated with a stock of a physical commodity. That commodity was firstly gold, then silver, and when these were scarce, copper was used. The attraction of physical money was that it is a 'real' asset, not a financial asset; it is a commodity rather than the liability of a bank.

The banking industry takes government-created or sponsored cash and uses it to create bank credit – loans to borrowers and to create bank deposits which are liabilities owed by banks. Bank deposit money, which is a claim to cash rather than cash itself – collaterised cash, if you like – is sometimes called 'fountain pen money' to reflect the fact that it is a creation of the banking industry.

The money supply can be narrowly or broadly defined. A narrow definition is just the stock of 'cash' in circulation and deposits at the central bank. A broad definition is the total stock of short-term liabilities issued by banks. The stock of liabilities is dynamic, meaning that it changes all the time. Money is created when a bank creates a new deposit against a new loan and destroyed when the loan is repaid. The total stock of money only increases when the banking industry as a whole increases its net deposits.

By definition, it is impossible to control the money supply, the total stock of shorter liabilities issued by banks, without also controlling the availability of credit from the banking system. Most of the time individual and independent borrowers and lenders tend to behave responsibly; that is, not borrow or lend too much. From time to time credit creates 'irrational exuberance', which leads to the creation of more credit.

Government is often the biggest single spender and borrower in an economy. It has enormous power to direct the central bank and the commercial banking system. 'Free market' policies discourage government from fully exploiting its powers. It is argued that poor credit judgements are made when the banking system does not have the freedom to decline loans, and that government borrowing crowds out other borrowers by taking up an excessive share of credit capacity. Socialist policies may sometimes explicitly use the banking system to further broader social objectives.

It does not sound to me as if government is in control of the money supply.

In complex systems it is rare that one player has absolute control. This is particularly the case in credit systems, which require the willing cooperation of borrowers and lenders. The fact that government has greater power than any other single player does not mean it can determine outcomes with any certainty.

Attempts to describe the relationships between the stocks and flows often resort to 'hydraulic' analogies, stocks and flows of water. One witty Heath Robinson cartoon shows the money supply as a pot of cold tea and economic activity as the flow of tea through the economy. Thinking of the money supply as a stock of water, say an alpine lake, captures key parts of reality. The water flowing into the lake is the new deposits created by the banking system. The water flowing out of the lake represents the deposits cancelled when bank credit is repaid. The overall level of the water in the lake is the result of countless different transactions. The overall consolidated result is hard to measure and to anticipate.

So, where do 'market forces' come into it?

'Market forces' is a shorthand expression to describe 'supply and demand' and they are the biggest factors in medium- and long-term interest rates. Of course, 'market forces' are not entirely self-organizing or spontaneous and their structure is greatly influenced by policy. Bagehot pointed out how different the structure of the banking industry was in England versus France or Germany in the 19th century. Current differences between the British, Japanese and Chinese systems are even greater. Basic facts like the amount of cash held per capita differ enormously between some countries, such as Japan *vis à vis* the UK.

So how does inflation come into all of this?

Inflation is a rise in the *general* level of prices. Supply and demand for most things varies, and price is usually the mechanism which brings the volumes supplied and demanded together. Fluctuations in prices are not necessarily inflationary.

The Monetarist explanation for inflation, often credited to Milton Friedman, is that inflation is caused by an increase in the money supply. As simplifications go, this is quite a good one.

The money supply can grow because either the central bank creates new cash through quantitative easing or because commercial banks collectively increase their lending. New central bank cash may not create any new credit if the QE cash is all spent buying existing assets. Buying existing assets, such as existing government bonds, may put their prices up. The rise in prices may have knock-on effects on other prices.

When commercial banks collectively increase their lending, they also create new deposits. Bad debts have an asymmetrical effect on loans versus deposits. Bad debts reduce the value of loans and their cost is borne by equity (solvency capital). Unless a bank goes bust, deposits are largely insulated from bad debts – by the equity and by explicit deposit guarantee schemes operated at an industry/system level. If the productivity of the stock of bank loans declines – because it is not ultimately repaid (bad debts) – then the value of the stock of bank money must depreciate over time. In other words, systematically making unproductive loans creates inflation. This is most obviously apparent in corrupt hyperinflationary regimes where the government instructs the central bank to print cash, which it spends indiscriminately. When governments finance current spending by borrowing and the money borrowed is not spent on productive assets or in ways that improve the productivity of the system, they dilute the quality of the overall stock of credit. Ultimately, such systematic dilution in credit quality also dilutes the value of money.

In theory, higher inflation should give rise to higher nominal interest rates. In practice, the time lag between action and reaction can often result in negative real interest rates.

So, what are 'real' rates of interest?

Real interest rates are the rates of interest earned after deducting the effect of general inflation. What is happening now in the wake of the Global Financial Crisis of 2008/09 is that there are several simultaneous effects on inflation:

1. The collective balance sheet of the commercial banking system is contracting to restore solvency and increase prudential ratios. By itself, all else being equal, this reduces the stocks of credit and money in the economy and is deflationary.

2. The central banks have grown their balance sheets by QE to compensate for the contraction of private bank credit.

3. Commodity prices, particularly commodities used for economic development like base metals and oil, are rising because of increased demand from

> Brazil, Russia, India and China. Soft commodity prices are rising as a result of world population growth and inelastic supply.

4. QE has driven up financial asset prices.

The net effect of this has been to create negative real interest rates at the short end of the yield curve. The deliberate intention behind this result is to restore the profitability of the banking system and to stimulate investment activity.

Central bank monetary policy seeks to steer a path between inflation and deflation – either of which can spiral out of control if they take hold. It might be said that policy after the Global Financial Crisis was designed to create short-term inflation to avert longer-term deflation.

So would I want to invest in 'financial assets'?

Yes, in most circumstances for at least part of your wealth. The only exception is when there is hyperinflation. If the rate of inflation is very high it becomes important to own real assets that offer the prospect of capital preservation.

Fortunately hyperinflation is relatively rare. It happens when the central bank is not independent of government and colludes in a form of tacit corruption. Systematic and prolonged creation of unproductive credit on the scale required to produce hyperinflation can only be achieved by deliberate deficit spending by government financed by central bank cash creation.

In times of low or moderate inflation, financial assets like cash and bonds have a number of advantages. They allow the investor to control the risks he is taking. For example, an investor can choose to hold cash or near cash. Cash offers no rate of return, but on the other hand involves very few short-term risks.[16]

---

[16] The main risk is currency devaluation.

An investor can determine the duration of his portfolio – fixing the repayment dates for his capital. Apart from cash, financial assets give stated nominal rates of return. In many countries governments give special tax advantages to domestic holders of government debt.

In short, financial assets allow precise financial engineering which an individual or business would normally find very hard to replicate at comparable cost.

I'm left with the impression that money and financial assets are to a large extent artificial!

That's because to a large extent they are. Money and financial assets are creations of civilisation. They are fantastic things. One of the fantastic things about them is that they allow civilisation to borrow from the future. So long as borrowings can be repaid, it works. In other words, it works so long as financial capital remains in touch with physical capital.

But it is not a complete representation of reality. For example, discounting cash works at a mathematical level. But if the cash is a representation of some sorts of real thing, it does not work. Can we discount a human life that is anticipated to start in 20 years' time at 10% per annum and say it is only worth 15% of a human life today?

Some features of the financial system are mythological – like the notion that government bonds are 'risk-free' or that cash has 'intrinsic value'. They are myths that apply or are true most of the time. But they are not absolute immutable truth.

Financial markets pursue 'financial value' or 'economic value' or cash with single-minded ruthlessness. Just occasionally, it does no harm to remember that the 'quest for value' is not purely about financial assets. Ultimately, returns on financial assets must correspond with the returns from real assets.

Safe Sex?

CHAPTER 5

The rate of return on 'real' assets

'We tell our people, "Don't worry about profit. Think about customer service." Profit is a by-product of customer service. It's not an end in and of itself.'
– Herb Kelleher, CEO *Southwest Airlines*

So, I think I've got the gist of returns on 'financial assets'. What about the returns on 'real' assets? How do we measure these?

Ultimately, all financial assets are derivatives of 'real' assets. The rate of return on financial assets must, in the long run, reflect the returns on real assets. Government can influence real returns over the long run, but it cannot determine them.

As we've seen, financial assets are defined in terms of money, have fixed durations and are, to a large extent, homogenous and 'fungible'. As a result, the market in financial assets is large and deep. The measurement of returns on real assets is much more difficult than the measurement of returns on financial assets.

Measuring, or perhaps more accurately 'discovering', the rate of return on real assets, let alone explaining it, is altogether more difficult.

Why are returns on real assets harder to measure?

There are loads of difficulties. What is the return you make on your house, for example? The answer depends on what value you impute to the right to live in your house – its imputed rental value – and on what you can sell it for at some point. The return on your house is not printed in a contract like the return on a bond.

The return on your house is likely to vary over time and in nominal terms. In some decades, your house might appreciate quite fast – especially if a major trunk road opens nearby to give access to a broader road network. In other decades, the value might stagnate. If the major source of employment in your area, say a coal mine, closes down then the value of your house might plummet. It might even become un-saleable.

The period over which you measure the returns is critical. Since returns 'overlap' so that, for example, the return after eleven years includes the returns in years one to ten, a few good or bad years may make a big difference.

Equities present particular problems.

Why are returns on equities more problematic?

The main reason is that equities have no fixed wind-up date. They are irredeemable securities.

If you tell me bonds are worth buying, we can quickly zero in on what sort of bond you are talking about. A bond is defined by its interest rate, duration, the priority or rank of its claim on the business or assets, and the quality of the issuer.

If you tell me equities are good value, it is more difficult to zero in on what your statement really means. Are you saying that equities are good value if held for one year, or five years or twenty-five years? Since equities have no explicit wind-up or repayment date, it is harder to know what you mean by good value.

So, how do we know what the return on equities is?

We don't know. It is not knowable in the sense that the nominal yield on a bond is knowable. It can only be estimated.

So, how do we *estimate* what the return on equities will be?

With greater difficulty than is often acknowledged. Professor Jeremy Siegel has sought an answer to this question and published a very successful book on the subject called *Stocks for the Long Run*. He examines stock data, prices, dividends, distributions and so on, for the USA in the 200-odd years since 1800.

His conclusion is that the best *estimate* of the average real return on equities over this period is 6.75% before investment management costs.

Professor Siegel's data is considered by some to be so remarkable as to set a benchmark. One well-known stock market economist, Andrew Smithers, refers to the long-run real average return of 6.75% as 'Siegel's "s"', something as close as one ever gets in economics to a theoretical constant.

Is that 'eureka'? Why wouldn't we just buy equities?
The 6.75% real is better than the returns we are currently getting on most financial assets.

Well, as you've guessed there are some major catches.

When one stands back from the data it is clear that Siegel has not discovered a constant ratio like π. (Nor does he claim as much.) The USA over this 200-year period may have been 'special' and therefore unrepresentative. It started the period in 1800 as a newly opened, under-populated continent. During the period, its rich resources of climate, waterways, coal, base metals and oil and gas were discovered and exploited. Cheap hydrocarbon energy drove productivity in every area from agriculture and transport to manufacturing and electronics. The US system of private property rights arguably incentivised faster exploitation of its natural and social resources than other property systems.

Like all averages this number, 6.75%, conceals as much as it reveals. What it does not tell us is the volatility of the returns. When volatility is considered, the return estimate can be refined to a probabilistic statement that we can be 90% sure that the average real returns over this period fell into the range 4.9% to 7.7%.

The main catch is that in order to get the average return, you have to invest over very long periods. And even if you did that, you would not *necessarily* get the average return. What the data shows is that if you invest in equities for periods of *not less than 20 years,* you should at least receive a positive real return. 'Positive real return' only means getting your money back in real terms. So the positive return even after 20 years might still be well below the 6.75% real shown by the history of the US equity markets since 1800.

So, even if the long-run average real return is 6.75%, we could still make a negative real return if we invested for a period of less than 20 years?

Yes! People selling index funds don't always point that out. Investors in Japanese equity indices since 1990 have had just that experience.

One of the difficulties with equities is that they do not have a fixed duration.

When they purchase equities, what duration or holding period do people assume?

Very hard to know! One way of getting around this is to work out what the return on equities purchased in a specific year would have been if they had been held for different durations.

A way of looking at this is to assume that everyone holds equities for periods *up to* 40 years. One person may be starting to save and may hold equities for a full forty years, another may already have been saving for one year and so hold equities for a full thirty-nine years and so on until we find someone who has already saved for thirty-nine years and will hold on for one more full year before retiring. Each will have a different holding period and return. But the simple average of the 40 different returns each holding period makes is representative of the returns achieved by investing in a given year.

Andrew Smithers has done these calculations. They show that there are some years which have been particularly bad years for investing in equities. Investing in 1928, 1929, 1967, 1968, 1969, 1971 and 1972 would not have yielded positive returns for ten years, and even after thirty years returns would not have reached the average long-run return.

So what does this show?

It shows that over very long periods – that is, greater than 20 years – the risk of absolute loss in equities as an asset class is very low. This is probably because equities as a class are real assets that keep their value in real terms. But over shorter periods, equities as a class are risky and give a range of real returns across a wide spectrum from negative to positive.

What determines the returns from equities for any given year, measured in the Smithers fashion? The biggest single factor is valuation. Smithers argues that it is related to the price paid in relation to the replacement cost of business assets. These variables can only be approximated and cannot be used for precise timing. The analysis shows that asset allocation is an important skill that can reduce risk and increase returns. The choices of financial assets versus real assets, and short duration assets versus long duration assets are very important.

Does that mean that you don't believe in 'stock picking'?

Stock picking has been out of fashion for many reasons. One is that the average equity fund manager underperforms the equity index. Another is that as soon as a portfolio includes ten or more stocks it tends to correlate with the market. So confidence that an index can be beaten is low.

And yet some stock pickers do beat the market and produce good returns. There are two elements of what they do. One is to find businesses with better returns; better in the sense of being higher returns on investment, and better in the sense of being sustained for longer periods. Another is that they buy these returns when the businesses are out of favour.

Identifying better returns is fundamental analysis. Identifying out-of-favour businesses is the knack of reading the market. This is a matter of judging its mood and having a feel for what most investors will find attractive and a matter of anticipating liquidity.

In many fields the test of the truth of a proposition is that it remains true, that is not falsified across time – possibly 'forever'. 'Truth' with equities is more ephemeral. Since an equity share is an irredeemable instrument, there is seldom a single 'moment of truth' when the underlying projects are liquidated allowing fundamental returns to be objectively measured. Instead equities 'travel hopefully but seldom arrive'. The fundamental performance of a business is ephemeral often on a short timescale and certainly on a longer historical scale. The market's enthusiasm for a business is also ephemeral.

So what is 'fundamental' analysis?

A cynic's definition might be 'whatever sells stocks'!

A serious-minded definition is that it is an enquiry into what returns a company can expect to make. Corporate returns depend on the investments made, the type of projects and the timing of the cash surpluses.

What investors are seeking is projects which can 'create value'. This means that the project takes $100 which could have been invested elsewhere at, say, a 5% return and achieves a return of at least 5%, thereby making the $100 invested worth at least $100. If the return achieved is greater than 5%, then the $100 becomes worth more than $100. How much more than $100 depends on both the margin achieved over and above the 5% and the length of time the margin can be sustained.

Fundamental analysis tries to work out whether the returns are likely to be higher or lower, and whether they beat some minimum rate required to compensate for the risks borne.

The ultimate goal of fundamental analysis is to work out if a company is fairly priced. This means distilling down the information to a judgement about the present value of the future cash surpluses that it is believed the company can generate.

'The long-run results we can discern in the data of stock market history are not a random set of numbers: each event was the result of a preceding event rather than an independent observation. This is a statement of the highest importance. Any starting conditions we select in the historical data cannot replicate the starting conditions at any other moment because the preceding events in the two cases are never identical. There is no predestined rate of return. There is only an expected return that may not be realised.'

– Peter Bernstein

CHAPTER 6

Fundamental analysis

'There is, I believe, a fundamental indeterminateness about the value of common shares even in principle. God Almighty does not know the proper price-earnings multiple for a common stock.'[17]

– Burton G Malkiel

So what determines the rate of return produced by a real asset or by a business?

Rates of return tend to follow certain predictable economic laws. One such law is the law of competition, which says that if there are many buyers and sellers of an undifferentiated product, there will be one market clearing price. In mature markets, competition tends to drive rates of return down to near the cost of capital unless the business has competitive advantages. So, on the whole, businesses with competitive advantages whose markets are not mature – that is, are still growing – give better returns than mature businesses without any competitive advantages.

---

[17] A Random Walk Down Wall Street, 1996

Competitive advantage

Which begs the question, what is a competitive advantage?

A competitive advantage is something which allows a business to be more productive, to get more out of every pound or dollar or euro it spends. There are many ways in which a business may legitimately do this and a few ways that are illegal. An illegal way would be collusion against the consumer, such as the creation of a price-fixing cartel. A straightforward competitive advantage is an economy of scale. Most businesses will have fixed costs. Sometimes most of the costs are fixed. If this is the case, a business which produces more units with the same fixed cost will have a lower cost per unit made and therefore be able to sell at a lower price, and so achieve a large market share, and so on. Another straightforward competitive advantage is innovation – making new things or old things in a new way, which is either patented or subject to proprietary know-how not available to the competitors.

How do you identify a business with a competitive advantage?

Most businesses do just one thing. Of course, businesses do gazillions of things as well. But usually the gazillions of things are all part of facilitating the 'just one thing'. The reason why most businesses do 'just one thing' is that to achieve product quality and cost competitiveness, a degree of specialisation of people, knowledge, equipment and process is required. The just one thing is a complex system of systems for delivering a particular sort of product to a particular sort of market. There may be many permutations and combinations of the product and the markets but they will tend to be variations around the same theme. Often it takes decades to accumulate and combine the skills required to do the just one thing. Of course, a company can own a collection of businesses. But each individual business typically focuses on doing just one thing.

So, for example, a life assurance company will sell savings products. That's the 'just one thing' which it does, just as assembling cars is what car companies do, generating electricity is what an electricity generating company does and selling 'bed nights' is what hotel companies do.

Any business is a system of systems. There are Human Resources systems to manage the employees, Customer Relationship Management systems to manage the sales and marketing, accounting systems to manage the numbers, production systems to manage manufacturing. Yet in any particular business, all the systems work together to create the 'just one thing'.

The 'just one thing' is usually non-trivial, specific and complex. Take electricity generation. There are multiple levels of granularity one can dig down into: the time profile and seasonality of demand, the structure of the company's cost curve, the market system for contracting for supply. In every business one can go down into the detail. Take the life assurance company. There is the structure of the savings products, the system for regulating the sale of the products and the company, the different channels through which the product is sold, the management of the assets that provide the returns.

When one abstracts from the detail and looks at the 'just one thing' and compares the way a company does that thing with the way other companies in the same industry do that thing, one discovers important differences. These are often differences in the customer segment addressed, the way the product is sold or the way it is put together. Many of the differences make no difference; the ones that are interesting are those that deliver increased productivity. Increased productivity may be productivity for the business – which allows it to make more at less cost and to pass on some of the cost benefit. It may also be increased productivity for the customer.

So competitive advantage is all about productivity?

Yes, if one had to find a one-word summary, productivity is probably about it. There is an entire bibliography of books on the subject to which the one word summary does no justice! What matters is the duration of the competitive advantage. Typically, competitive advantage is a 'wasting asset' because the world always moves on and the competition is continuously seeking out new ways of increasing productivity. The beauty (and the curse) of the market system is that a business cannot rest on its laurels, but has to improve continuously – a process the Japanese have given the name 'Kaizen'. Productivity is not a thing, but a process. We are mainly interested in prospective and potential productivity. Of course, the future productivity may be made possible because of past actions and achievements – such as having built up a large installed base of customers. And the productivity may be achieved as much, if not more, by how the business operates in its industry as by what it does. So a business may achieve productivity gains by not having certain key processes in-house (inside its own system of systems), and by leveraging on other companies' processes.

A life assurance company might decide not to have a sales force and only to sell through other companies, for example. A car assembler might decide not to make certain subsystems (say brakes, electronics or tyres). How the business is configured will depend on where the economies of scale in each of the subsystems can be achieved. It often turns out that the capacity utilisation of the system of systems is constrained by one of the subsystems. So production might be the constraint, and building a new production line might require huge investment. Or, sales might be the constraint and it might be relatively difficult to double the size of the sales force. Understanding how the 'system of systems' scales reveals how productivity might increase.

So it is also about anticipating change?

The 'just one thing' may not change much, but the way it is produced may change dramatically. So a railway company in 2008 is demonstrably in the same sort of business as a railway company in 1908. But the way the just one thing is delivered, and what the subsystems within the system of systems may be, and how they interact, have changed beyond recognition. In railways, the locomotive technology changed (from coal/steam to diesel and electric) and the composition of the system of systems changed (train operating companies no longer own the trains or the tracks in the UK, for example). The market for transportation also changed beyond recognition during the hundred years as modes of transport which hardly existed in 1908 – such as cars, trucks and planes – became substitutes for rail transportation.

Likewise, a restaurant in 1908 and in 2008 is recognisably the same sort of business. But the methods of production have been revolutionised. Productivity improvements across all the component systems in the system of systems have increased the quantity and quality of restaurant meals prodigiously. Refrigeration played a large part. To increase productivity, repeatability and scale-ability, the focus in catering has moved from cooking to assembly.

The law of paradox applies: there is nothing new under the sun and everything is new under the sun. New technology makes it possible to do the same things in completely new and more efficient ways, and it makes it possible to do things which were previously impossible.

The trouble with all of this is that it seems impossible to anticipate all the changes. They just can't be quantified.

No, they cannot be quantified precisely. But they can be estimated. As J.M. Keynes said, it is better to be roughly right than precisely wrong. One can think of a business as a project. The project has a natural 'life' and then life extensions and evolutions. Life of the project normally means life of the investment, that is the real capital deployed, rather than the life of the market or the resource. But it may be that project life is also constrained by the market or the resource. Fashion or technology changes may determine the life of a market. The size of an ore body may determine the life of a mining project.

Business as a project

How does thinking about a business as a project help?

A moment ago we talked about a business as doing 'just one thing'. In order to isolate and understand the economics of the 'just one thing' it helps to distil down the detail and produce an abstract model that describes the archetypal project that the business manages.

A business is, as we discussed, a project of projects. We can't and don't wish to model all the projects that combine to make up 'the' project. If a defence contracting business works on a secret defence project for the government, for example, even the chief executive of the business may not know the precise nature of the product. Even if information on the sub-projects is available, we may not need to look at it or to understand it. It is not necessary to understand how to build a hotel or an aeroplane in order to build a model of the basic economics of a project to manage a hotel or airline. It is not necessary to know the fine detail of how a jet engine works or is designed in order to create a model of the economics of a project to build jet engines. Of course, it helps to have access to people who do understand such things, but one does not have to be an expert oneself.

An example would really help me understand here!

Okay, let's take a business that's quite easy to understand – a hotel. A hotel is all about capacity: rooms and room nights and capacity utilisation. Many businesses that manage a stock of installed capacity – say hotels, planes or people – have the same characteristic. Returns relate to managing capacity and capacity utilisation. An individual hotel usually operates several distinct projects – 1) selling room nights; 2) selling food and beverages; and 3) selling additional services (such as conference facilities). Most of the capital in the project is sunk in the hotel rooms. An individual hotel scales on the number of rooms. Increasing the number of rooms in some hotels is quite easy, and in some next to impossible. A hotel group scales by adding hotels. The archetypal projects in the hotel business for which one needs to build an economic model are therefore an individual room and an individual hotel. It turns out in the hotel industry that different sorts of hotels have different sorts of rooms and different economics. So at one end of the market there are 'luxury/upscale', 'full service' hotels, and at the other end of the market there are no-frills budget hotels. A full service hotel has very different economics – requiring a higher upfront capital investment, for example, and greater fixed costs to operate. The land, the building and the minimum level of staffing for a full service hotel are all higher than for a budget hotel, but in the right location will provide returns about as good as a budget hotel chain.

Doesn't your hotel project depend on a whole lot of other projects over which you have little control?

Yes, and the extent of the interdependence varies. It depends on the project. Every project will depend on other projects and often the biggest assumptions are that the larger supporting projects will deliver as required.

Suppose you won the franchise from the government to provide a train service from London to, say, Liverpool. Typically this project might be quite short term – say five to ten years. This project would depend on several other overarching projects – many of them projects with much longer lives – say 30 years.

It would require a project to provide the tracks – in a given state of repair and availability. It would require a project to deliver electricity for the trains – of a certain quality and availability. It would require a project to provide trains. Since you only have a five-year franchise, say, you are not going to buy the trains outright. So you need someone to finance the trains and lease them to you.

If any one of the overarching projects fails, your franchise will probably fail. It may not fail financially, because you may have contracted in such a way with your suppliers to lay off much of the risk. But it will not flourish.

If you wish to operate the trains then you will not wish or be able to be expert in the mysteries of track maintenance, electricity supply and so on. So you will subcontract these elements. In a developed market there may be market prices for these services where many contracts have already been agreed over the years by many people. You will wish to concentrate on your areas of comparative advantage – attracting customers, motivating staff, building a brand.

If you are operating on a frontier – often literally as in a mining project – you may have to build the supporting long-term projects as well. To bring your mine into production in the Congo, say, you may need to build at least some of the roads, much of the power generation and all of the accommodation for the workers, for example.

Don't you have to make rather a lot of assumptions to create such an archetypal project model?

Yes. The projects are all interlinked. How the linkages work is not apparent to most of the players. It may appear that the projects form a cascade – that the train franchise project depends on the electricity supply contract, which in turn depends on the government. Cascade implies hierarchy. Everyone is familiar with hierarchy – it is sort of a natural condition deriving from the age profile of the population. People who have been around longer have more knowledge and more power. We have all been to school!

And yet, although there is some hierarchy in the pattern of interlinkages, there's also interdependence of the largest project on the smallest project, and vice versa. One more or one less passenger will not break the franchise project. But over a period, 15% fewer passengers against the expectation might easily break the franchise project.

What are the key links between the projects? Clearly the prices and the contracts that determine how they interlink. So the train franchise operator needs to contract with a lessor to get hold of trains. The reliability of the price and the contract are the essential prerequisites for the chain to work. In a market system, the prices are dynamically set and re-set by many people operating in many circumstances as the contracts are each negotiated and renewed and renegotiated many times over the years. The lawyers introduce new terms into the agreements as new factors arise. In a centrally planned system some person or team has to assume almost God-like knowledge to try to determine how the different projects should interlink.

Aren't some projects easier to 'project' than others?

Yes, the amount of heroism required to make the assumptions varies from industry to industry. Suppose we compare the hotels and airline projects. Both businesses manage a stock of capital equipment – hotels and planes. Hotels have pretty stable business models. The basic product has not changed much over time and the key assumptions, like the life of the hotel, can be forecast quite reliably.

The units on which an airline scales are 'seat miles', planes and landing slots or routes. One wants to have a model of the economics of the archetypal seat mile. The main costs are depreciation (c.20% of annual costs), staff (c.25%), and fuel (c.12–20%). Operating margins vary from zero to 5% for a national-flag-carrier-full-service airline to around 20–25% for a low-cost airline.

Most of the assumptions required to run the model for a plane are more uncertain than they are for a hotel. The price of aviation fuel, which fell in real terms from 1980 to 2002, rose rapidly in 2007. One needs to take some view of oil prices. The life of a plane is more subject to technological obsolescence than a hotel. One needs to take a view on new plane developments – fortunately, the lead times to create a new plane are long. Staff are more highly unionised in the airline industry and have greater bargaining power.

How do you make these assumptions?

In a variety of ways; you can try to isolate the most critical assumptions and do some fundamental analysis of the price history and the structure of supply and demand.

Of course, life is too short to do this on the entire chain of supporting projects. So you have to have faith in at least some of the market prices.

You can consult an expert. Every industry will have 'an expert', someone who gathers and publishes information. There is, for example, a large business-to-business publishing industry that does exactly this. In some industries, the companies themselves poll their customers and publish annual studies of supply and demand. Boeing, Airbus and Rolls-Royce periodically publish studies and forecasts of demands for planes, for example.

Most of the time, most people assume the near future will follow the same trend as the near past.

In large parts of the world superstition plays a big part. Don't laugh! If there isn't a mental model to explain how the pieces fit together, if there's very limited information and little control over life, people consult the witch doctor or the clairvoyant. Some of the largest and most profitable pay-by-the-minute phone services are for astrological predictions. Astrology is a big business.

Supply and demand

How do we do the fundamental analysis of supply and demand?

A good place to start is with the experts. They have done a lot of the 'heavy lifting' – in terms of gathering information and defining the variables.

When one studies market forecasts, it soon emerges that everything is circular! This does not mean that it is not forecastable. It simply means that to arrive at an accurate forecast one has to think in terms of the sustainability of the whole system.

To illustrate the point about circularity, consider how you would forecast the demand for planes or cars. The abstract thing that people buy when they buy planes and cars is transport. The practical thing that plane makers and auto makers supply is a machine which delivers miles per person – that is seat miles. A 500-seat plane delivers twice the seat miles of a 250-seat plane – no wonder planes are built bigger and bigger. To work out how many planes the world will demand, one needs to make an assumption about how many seat miles people will wish to purchase.

In reality, demand for seat miles depends on a host of factors – like the cost of seat miles (cost of plane over life, and fuel and staff), the availability of airports, the carbon cost of air travel if ever paid for by the passengers, the cost of substitutes like video conferencing, average levels of income and leisure, and so on.

In practice, the forecasters make a stab at these issues and condense everything into one factor or a small number of factors to which they can correlate seat miles. So, in a one-factor model, annual seat miles will be plotted against annual Gross Domestic Product (GDP). And over time, statistical relationships can be observed. Seat miles rise with incomes and infrastructure. Changes in GDP have a leveraged relationship with changes in seat miles.

We can take a look at changes in GDP over some long period and at changes in seat miles, or Revenue Passenger Kilometres (RPKs) as they are called in the industry, over some long period and look to see if there is some relationship.[18]

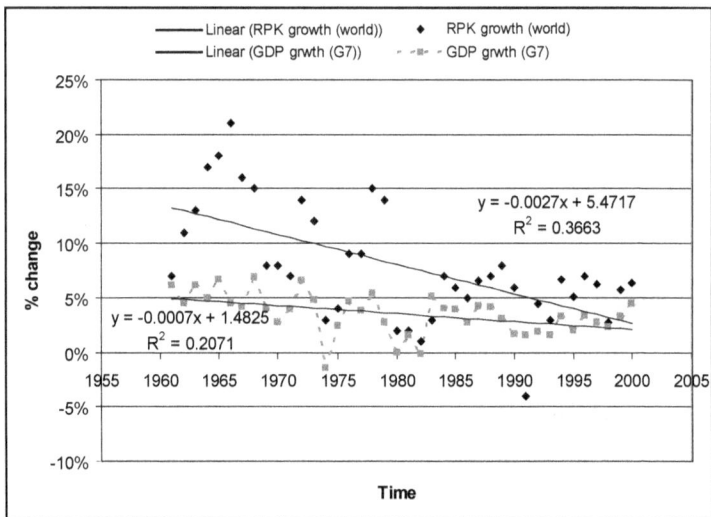

Looking at this historic data, we can see that RPKs have grown twice as fast as GDP. But this two-times multiplier has been falling over time as the industry matures.

---

[18] The chart and data are reproduced with the kind permission of Nick Cunningham, a veteran airlines analyst at Agency Partners, www.agencypartners.co.uk.

If we have an opinion or forecast for GDP we can predict RPK growth. With a view of RPK growth and knowledge of the RPK capacity of different aircraft, with a view of the mix of RPKs (that is, short haul versus long haul and so on), and with a view of the age structure of the existing fleet of planes, it is possible to forecast how many new planes will be required. You can see that the model can get complicated and detailed quite quickly.

A forecast is achieved. The requirements of the client have been met. Demand has been correlated with GDP and there are plenty of other experts who forecast GDP.

When one stands back from this, one can see that the causal thinking has not got around the fact that everything depends on everything else – it is just that everything else has been called GDP. The model meets its objectives: it gives quantitative outputs which influence, if not determine, production decisions. It works in the short term because the forecasting period is so short in relation to the life of the system. It therefore gives psychological comfort.

Paradox applies here: to forecast the short term one has to have a view of the long term, and the long term is itself made up of all of the short terms. Everything depends on everything else and yet it is possible to come up with accurate forecasts which apply for quite long periods of time, certainly years and sometimes decades.

So, can we trust the experts?

Often you can trust their data. One has to be more wary about their conclusions. Most experts are not disinterested philanthropists. They are working for someone. It would be too cynical to say that this always distorts their judgement. But it must colour it. This is why a key qualification for an investor is the ability to take an independent view. That sounds easy but in practice is difficult. Experts are supported with data and dignity. Governments are supported by gravitas and by the media and by millions of dollars. And you beg to differ? It is easy to disdain the contrarian view but truth is not a respecter of rank. The little boy, not the ministers, saw that the emperor was naked. Paradox applies. It is not necessarily necessary to be an expert to identify that the experts may be wrong. So long as I have seen a table that is plumb, level and square I can tell you if a particular table is likely to be any good as a table. I don't have to be able to make the table myself.

To ask a plane maker to forecast that demand for planes will fall is a bit like asking a butcher if you should eat meat. Even if the butcher is privately a vegetarian, he's unlikely to tell you. It would be bad for business. Plane makers make planes, car makers make cars, cigarette makers make cigarettes – and bankers make loans – that's the organisational imperative. Such organisations are unlikely to be led by people who do not believe that their products are 'good' or by people who forecast the decline of the product.

This is not to say that disinterested philanthropists make better forecasters than the businesses which make the products, or that a business with falling sales volumes may not be a good investment. The point is simply that a system has a certain momentum and trajectory and it gains its direction partly because most people believe in it. The trick is to find a trend or an inflection point.

Does that mean we should look for tipping points?

The installed base of different technologies grows and shrinks. Tipping points happen when the growth rates or decline rates accelerate sharply. This happens because once certain thresholds are crossed, whole systems become unsustainable. A simple example would be an engineering product that has been in decline for many years. As unit volume shrinks, each unit has to bear a greater share of the business overhead. Overhead can be cut to a certain point. When finally the unit volume falls below the threshold needed to support the scale of a particular machine, say, the product is abruptly discontinued. Given the very small fleet of planes in service, the loss of an Air France Concorde on take-off in Paris significantly reduced the installed base of planes. Increased costs per unit was presumably one of the factors taken into account when Airbus decided to discontinue engineering support for the supersonic passenger jet.

To describe this process in large complex systems, people use the mountain of sand analogy. Imagine a constant flow of sand poured onto the same spot. A pile quickly forms. The height of the pile does not grow continuously in proportion to the flow of sand. Occasionally, the pile of sand abruptly collapses.

Sometimes some observers can see that the risk of a collapse in the pile of sand or in unit volumes is above average. They then put bets on this happening – which, with some variables, may make it more likely to happen. This happened when some observers understood that sterling's membership of the European Exchange Rate Mechanism in 1992 was unsustainable. The economic cycle in the UK was out of phase with the cycle in Germany. The UK needed lower interest rates, and Germany, higher. Some observers, famously George Soros, bet that the system would fail. They sold Sterling in the belief that the UK government would not be able to sustain the high interest rates needed to support the currency within the Exchange Rate Mechanism. Although the UK was close to recession the government raised interest rates to defend the exchange rate. UK interest rates momentarily reached 17% before the government abandoned the Exchange Rate Mechanism. The speculators made money when Sterling was devalued.

The skill is to see if there are any trends in the industry or in demand which will persist, or to see if there is a cycle which will repeat or at least rhyme.

Most industries have cycles and most have certain directional trends. Quite often these trends persist for many years. One of the trends in the hotel industry in the last 20 years has been increasing concentration of hotels into common marketing groups or common ownership. In 1996 'brands' accounted for around 30% of hotel beds in the UK and that proportion has risen over time. Hotel ownership and branding has grown progressively more concentrated to achieve economies of scale in marketing. Another trend has been the roll-out of low-cost, provincial, budget hotels. In the airline industry, the big trend of the last ten years has been the expansion of the no-frills, low-cost airlines.

Trends that persist for long periods in industries tend to involve the introduction of productivity tools and additional capacity. Often the two go hand in hand – the productivity gain reduces costs, which are passed on to the consumer, which increases the size of the market. Budget hotels and low-cost airlines are more productive – they deliver more bed nights and air miles at lower costs –and have attracted more users.

So, we should invest in new productivity trends?

Adoption of new products and productivity tools tend to follow an 'S-curve'. It takes a long time – sometimes decades – for the product to get adopted in a few niche markets. Then it goes through a period of very rapid volume growth as it moves into a mass-market, high-volume phase. Finally, once the market is saturated when the potential customer base is fully penetrated, volumes produced fall. Cars have gone through the entire S curve in Western Europe. They started as products for a niche of wealthy consumers. Then unit volume grew rapidly as cars became a mass-market product. Finally, unit volume stagnated when the market was fully penetrated. For some products, the S-curve takes place over such a long period that it is hardly noticed. For technology products the adoption rate is so fast that they are clearly visible. S-curves can be plotted for the roll-out of analogue radios, televisions, personal computers or mobile phones.

It is not sufficient for success to invest in a new technology trend. Timing is everything. Investing in the bottom half of the S-curve can be a long and laborious experience of funding and refunding the project. And to reap the rewards one has to persevere up the S-curve when many investors have been shaken out.

A different way of playing technology roll-outs is not to time the position of the market on the S-curve, but to invest in parallel S-curves. So if one knows that mobile phones have been adopted in Europe, it may be a safe inference that they will be adopted in an emerging market – say, Egypt or Nigeria. Similarly, if one knows that a productivity tool has been adopted in one industry, it may be possible to infer safely that it will be adopted in a different industry.

How do you go from an archetypal project to a business?

The difference between a project and a business is that a project is seldom expected to continue indefinitely, whereas a business is. Some projects have very long lives. A plane, or at least its airframe, may have a physical life of 30 years. A hotel may have a life of 100 years, an aircraft carrier 50 years, a railway 100 years plus. These are so long in relation to a human life that people think of them as indefinite. But they are not, and the people who design them make realistic estimates about how long the component parts may last and how often they need to be replaced. One of these long-life assets is itself a rolling sequence of projects that successively renews the overall project. So within the life of one plane, which one might think of as one project, there is a sequence of overhaul projects to overhaul or replace the engines, software systems, electronic control systems and so on.

So, for example, a mining company will start off with a plan for a project to build a mine with an expected life of, say, 20 years. The resource being mined may be large enough to still be mined in 100 years. But the project initially has a 20-year life. Within the overall project, there will be sub-projects, projects to invest capital in sinking a new shaft or building new winding gear, or projects to add new capacity to treat more ore. As the end of the 20 years approaches, extensions to the project will be considered. These may include investing capital to prove up more mineable resource. The original project may be extended indefinitely provided that the market for the resource, coal or iron or some other metal is still demanding product; that the geological resource has not run out; and that the mine is still economic – that is, can produce at a market competitive price. Something similar would apply to a hotel, a ship or a power station.

Yet although projects may repeat and continue for very long periods – maybe for several generations – they are generally expected to stop at some point – if not by design then by virtue of changes in external circumstances. Hotels, planes, ships and power stations are very often not taken out of commission because they don't work any more, but because new technologies have been discovered and made economic more productive ways of achieving the same result.

Some businesses are set up to manage specific projects and their lives are synchronous with the project. Most businesses, though, are incorporated as companies and have no finite wind-up date. People just expect the companies to continue – particularly if they are large and have large bureaucracies. This belief arises partly from inertia, partly from laziness and partly because some companies do successfully reinvent themselves.

There is a glorious roll call of companies which reinvented themselves – bicycle repair shops that turned into motor car retailers and manufacturers, high street grocers that turned into multinational supermarket chains (J Sainsbury), chemical companies that turned into pharmaceutical products businesses (ICI/Zeneca). A particularly remarkable example is the wood and pulp mill business named after the Nokia River in Finland on which it built a pulp mill, and which is now the leader in the mobile phone business.

There's also a roll call of companies that stopped, some very abruptly and some which died very slowly. Ferranti was a company with a long history in electrical products, radar and defence systems. It purchased a US defence contractor called International Signal & Control in 1987, only to discover that ISC's order book was largely fraudulent. When this was discovered, the business abruptly went bust. British Coal Corporation was a business incorporated by the British Government in 1947 to buy out/nationalise Britain's coalfields. As the price of sea transport declined and as giant opencast coal fields were opened up in places like South Africa, Australia and the USA most of British Coal's underground mines became uncompetitive and were only closed after years of political and social strife. British Coal Corp was wound up in 1997.

And how does the project 'evolve'?

It evolves by achieving the same or similar end results by using different means. Every industry provides examples. Take the savings industry. When life companies started off in the 18th century they started selling life assurance contracts, that is contracts which paid out when the customer died on the basis of the then 'new new thing' – statistical analysis of life expectancy. In Victorian England they then got into savings policies for the middle classes. These were sold door-to-door by salesmen on commission. The savings products all shared in a common pool of investments – the 'life fund' and the returns were allocated to individual policies by an actuary. Over time as technology changed the method of selling, the product changed so that door-to-door selling became a smaller and progressively less competitive part of the business. Other channels, such as direct marketing, selling the product through channels such as estate agents and independent financial advisers and, recently, the internet, became more important. As financial markets evolved and computer technology became cheaper, it became cost effective to offer a disintermediated product: product in which the returns were directly related to the underlying investments ('unitised') so that the life company gave no minimum guaranteed return. The underlying conceptual product – a savings product turning income into capital – has remained the same across the centuries. But the technology for constructing and selling the product has changed almost completely.

Project 'extensions' and 'evolutions'

How does understanding project 'extensions' and 'evolutions' help choose good companies in which to invest?

It helps because the essential profitability of the underlying project and its scaleability determine the overall profitability of the business and often the whole industry. Most projects have a finite maximum output and therefore value. A 20-megawatt power station has a maximum 'name plate' or design capacity. Maximum capacity utilisation is so many hours a day for so many days a year, allowing for downtime for essential maintenance. Some plants operate well within capacity because demand, or distribution, or price is constrained. Some sort of similar calculation applies to most businesses that provide services by operating stocks of equipment or people such as aeroplanes, machines, or lawyers or engineers. If one can establish what the intrinsic profitability of one unit is then one can make inferences about how many units the market might support, how the competition might respond, how firms might choose to compete and where margins might end up. The more novel the technology, the greater the productivity gains it delivers, and the newer the business the more difficult it is to assess how profitable a project may be. But then the reward for making the right inference is much greater if one understands the 'roll-out' path for a new machine than for building one more unit for a mature market.

Tell me more about project evolutions.

Projects are very interesting because they evolve in unpredictable ways. The history of every industry is full of discoveries of new ways to improve productivity. Take the oil industry. There was a need to find cheaper ways of finding oil than drilling many dry holes. One of these was the development of seismic technology to determine the geology many meters and kilometres beneath the surface. Seismic technology works by making inferences about the different layers of rock below the surface by measuring the time it takes for sound waves to be reflected back up to the surface by the different geological strata. Seismic technology replaced one problem, lack of information, with another, too much data. Huge quantities of data needed to be processed and interpreted to make meaningful geological inferences. The oil industry's investment in seismology in part funded the development of the computing power to process the data, which in turn led to development of the first silicon chips. Texas Instruments is still one of the world's biggest silicon chip makers.

Some project extensions involve much larger leaps away from the original business. A private civil engineering business owned by a British entrepreneur called Weetman Pearson first discovered oil in Mexico. This came about because Pearson's contracting firm won the contracts to build the canal to drain Lake Texcoco around Mexico City, and later the contract to build the inter-ocean railway across the country from the Atlantic to the Pacific. In the course of travelling to these projects across the USA from New York, the train stopped in Texas and Pearson learned of the oil discoveries there. He subsequently applied for and was granted licences to explore for oil in Mexico, and spent huge amounts of his personal fortune (some £5m in 1909) drilling for oil in Mexico and his discoveries effectively founded the oil industry in Mexico.

In one case, projects to process oil industry seismic data gave rise to projects to develop new electronic hardware, including the silicon chip. In the other case, the local infrastructure put in place to build a railway line was redeployed to explore for oil. What these project extensions illustrate is how private capital and entrepreneurs seek to meet continually evolving needs, needs which a central planner would struggle to learn of, let alone predict or anticipate. The 'jobsworths' in the central planning hierarchy would struggle even harder to take on the risk. Project evolutions are options to satisfy new needs or to develop and exploit new markets. This sort of option is known as a 'real option' to distinguish it from a financial option. A real option is exercised by executing a business strategy and a financial option is exercised by taking up a right to buy or sell.

CHAPTER 7

Generic business projects and archetypal business models

'When first we meant to build,
We first survey the plot, then draw the model.'
– Shakespeare, *Henry IV, Pt 2, I iii*

'"Theories without facts may be barren, but facts without theories are meaningless."'
– Kenneth Boulder

'...important characteristics of maps should be noted. A map is not the territory it represents, but, if correct, it has a similar structure to the territory, which accounts for its usefulness.'
A. Korzybski, *Science & Sanity*

You've gone into a lot of detail to explain what you mean by a business 'project'. I get lost in the detail. Is there any way of abstracting some enduring patterns from the mass of information?

I think there is. It helps to know what sort of 'animal' you are looking at without knowing all the details of how it lives. I think business projects fall into a small number of archetypal activities. In Business as in Fiction there are some basic plots. Most business projects fall into more than one 'pure' archetypal model. But one archetype tends to typify what the project does more than the others.

So what are these archetypal business models?

To get any economy going there must be two basic activities. You can't work out which comes first. They are both essential. There must be some form of credit and some sort of supply of natural resources. Finance business models and resources business models are two archetypal business models.

Finance business models

Tell me about finance business models.

We talked earlier about capital and defined it by reference to time as a stock of stuff which endures over many accounting periods. Stocks of capital take two generic forms, which we have also talked about: capital in the form of real assets, real capital if you like; and capital in the form of money, very broadly defined, which we can call financial capital.

Finance business models create and manage stocks of financial assets. Financial assets are all based on credit. Credit in its broadest sense is simply taking deferred payment. Everybody gives and takes credit. The essence of credit is that a claim is granted which can be exercised in the future. This requires a degree of trust and the rule of law. Without a legal system and ownership rights, financial assets cannot be created – we are just reduced to bartering what we have for what we need.

What is it that is 'archetypal' about finance business models?

Money and credit. These are the products that finance business models individually and collectively create and manage. Money and credit are means of managing resources and moving them between economic units and across time.

So what are the main types of finance business?

They fall into three broad categories: banking, investing and insuring. All finance business models use financial assets to move resources between economic units and across time. The banking industry uses loans to make resources available today against repayment in the future. The pensions industry creates pools of financial assets to create income in the future. The insurance industry makes capital available to customers if they suffer a predefined loss.

Do they differ much?

In theory, they are all doing something similar: making financial capital available in some form. In practice, they are very different.

What's particular about banking?

To supply credit systematically is a specialist business activity. The classic business model is 'on-balance sheet' lending and the activity is generically referred to as banking. The organisations doing the banking may go by different names. So there are banks, building societies, savings and loans companies, hire purchase companies, leasing companies, credit card companies and so on. But they are all lending.

On-balance sheet lending is the business of co-creating loans with customers. The loans are bank credit – money owed *to* banks. The commensurate amount owed *by* banks is money.

What is so special about bank credit that makes it the collateral for money?

I suppose the answer in one word is liquidity. Banks' credit is more liquid than the credit created by most sectors of the economy. The liquidity of bank credit results from some key features. One is that all the banks in a given monetary system are networked. All the banks are connected directly or indirectly with each other through inter-bank markets and with the central bank, just as all the computers on a network are connected to a central server, as it were. Another is that the duration of bank credit is known and managed. Many assets may earn higher rates of return than bank credit, but since they are not as liquid, they are not as 'bankable'.

Banks do a lot of things which are not traditional 'on-balance sheet' lending. They also create, issue, sell and trade financial assets. These may be traditional financial assets like bonds and currencies and more complex contracts like options, swaps, contracts for differences and futures. 'Securitisation' has been a huge growth area for banks. Whereas traditional on-balance sheet lending is constrained by the requirement to hold solvency capital against the risk that the assets might lose value over their remaining lives, securitisation is an intermediary business – like being an estate agent – and requires very little capital.

What about the 'savings and investment' industry? Is that different from banking?

The main difference is one of timescale. Banking mainly deals with financial assets that are 'bankable'; in other words, convert to cash on a relatively shorter timescale and with very high degrees of certainty. By definition, these financial assets are mainly debt securities of one form or another.

The savings and investment industry deals with longer timescales or durations, mainly because the main purpose of savings for most people is to create a pot of financial capital to support them in old age – to provide a pension.

The savings industry accumulates assets out of income in the near term to create a pool of financial capital in the long term. It also does the reverse. It takes financial capital and converts it back into a stream of income by providing annuities.

Asset accumulation products include pensions and unit trusts. Government often creates tax incentives to save. So products that include an element of life assurance get favourable tax treatment. The life assurance industry sells asset accumulation products with life and pensions 'bells and whistles'.

The further out in time one travels, the more unpredictable the outcomes. Paradoxically a debt security like a bond, which has very certain cashflows over short durations, may have rather risky cashflows over very long durations. This is less because the nominal cashflows are risky, but more because there is the risk that the real value of money declines. Some sorts of equity security by contrast may have risky cashflows over short durations, but provide less risky cashflows over longer durations. This could be because the underlying business is a 'real asset', which supplies and regularly re-prices an enduring product.

And insurance. I thought that was about risk rather than capital?

Well, it's about both. The natural ecosystem and the economic ecosystem are risky places: tectonic plates move, rivers flood, lightning strikes; borrowers default, currencies disappear, technologies fail. Many of these risks are insurable. The prerequisite for insurance is financial capital. Insurance is the business of making financial capital available to customers in the event that they suffer a financial loss. Insurers write contracts in which they take premiums from customers in exchange for underwriting defined potential losses over defined periods. The customers get access to the insurers' balance sheets in the event that they need to make a claim, and the insurers are effectively lending out their capital to customers who cannot afford to take the hit of a substantial loss.

Resources business models

What are the archetypal features of resources business models?

Resources are part of the natural ecosystem. They are 'real' physical stuff. They are physically discovered – like a coal seam. Resources, like God, *are* existence and they are ultimately a mystery.

What gives resources a value? Do resources have an 'intrinsic value'?

Resources are where the 'objective' realities of material existence confront human ingenuity. Resource economics are not black and white. There's paradox and there are large grey areas. So on the one side, there is the physical and apparently 'objective' reality of how much stuff is 'out there'. And on the other side, there are the subjective requirements of civilisation and the economic ecosystem and the availability of credit.

Classical economics has it that relative abundance and scarcity determines relative value. So fresh air is free in most places because abundant[19] and fresh water is free in some places and in others costs money.

For the most part, the economic value of resources is superimposed by the economic ecosystem, which reflects human requirements for particular resources at particular times. It depends partly on timescale. In the short term, relative supply and demand is paramount. In the long run, the environment has an intrinsic value in terms of quality of life, which the economic pricing mechanism has great difficulty measuring in money terms.

If resources have 'intrinsic' value it is of a metaphysical rather than a monetary nature – the beauty of the natural ecosystem, of all the creatures in it and of how it all works together.

---

[19] Fresh air can be bought in shops in Tokyo and elsewhere.

So what determines abundance and scarcity?

Supply and demand. These come down to a combination of factors. One is the natural endowment of the resource and the form in which it appears. Another is the technology for finding, processing and using the resource or a substitute resource. Another is how civilisation believes the resource should be used and husbanded. All of these factors are evolving all the time.

Supply and demand for some resources are remarkably stable for very long periods of time, which gives an impression of stability. Other resources go from abundance to scarcity and back with surprising speed.

The economics of some resources can be particularly brutal. The supply of the resource may be difficult to increase in the short term and may require massive capital investment. Supply is therefore said to be inelastic. The demand for the resource may depend on sales of capital goods, which is cyclical and greatly influenced by the credit cycle. The combination of lumpy supply, high fixed costs that are largely irrecoverable or 'sunk', and cyclical demand creates the conditions for volatile prices.

How reliable is supply and demand in creating the 'right' price?

Hmmm. Is there a 'right' price? Rightness in economics is usually about having the right stuff in the right place at the right time. Supply and demand is usually rather good at creating prices for getting stuff to places on relatively short timescales. Where it can break down is where supply and demand only change over long time periods. Long time periods and long lead times are more difficult because they require long-term planning. An example of long-term planning that failed was the South African electricity generation and distribution system in the 2000s. Eskom, the national power company, and the government failed to invest sufficiently in new capacity to supply new demand. As a result, there are significant shortages of electricity and blackouts.

So why isn't demand for something like electricity
correctly anticipated?

Many reasons. One reason is politics with a small 'p'. The process
for creating policy may be ineffective. The ultimate decision
makers – politicians – may just not understand the problem.

Another reason is that the information systems may be giving
false readings or may be corrupted. An important factor is
whether a profit is correctly calculated. For example, if a
national electricity company overstates profits by not using
replacement costs to calculate the costs of supply then the
consequences may be that the electricity is under-priced.
Under-pricing distorts supply and demand, too much profit is
paid out to shareholders (the government), and too little cash
is reinvested in capacity.

Another reason is that prices alone do not necessarily give
sufficient information on which to make a decision. Economics
gives the impression that all resources are equally important
because it reduces everything to pure money values. In practice,
though, there is a general hierarchy of importance and some
of the resource 'ingredients' for modern civilisation are more
critical than others.

How do you rank the importance of resources?

Some resources are essential and others nice to have. At the top
of the list are water and energy. Food is a subset of energy and
water. These key resources are the preconditions for civilisation
and human life. Again paradox applies. Energy resources
are at once finite and super-abundant. So on the one hand,
hydrocarbons from fossil fuels (coal, oil and gas) are finite
resources. And on the other hand, the daily inflow of solar
energy is enormous and dwarfs human consumption.

How important is energy?

Exceptionally. From an historical perspective, changes in technology for capturing and using energy have driven changes in the whole structure of civilisation.

Most energy derives from the sun. The sun drives photosynthesis, the process by which plants combine the hydrogen in water with carbon dioxide from the air to create 'carbohydrates' such as sugars, from which starches and oils can be derived. Carbohydrates trap solar energy, or rather convert solar energy into latent chemical energy. When the carbohydrates are broken down by digestion or burning, the energy is released again. The sun also drives the climate system, which creates wind and wave energy.

When the carbohydrates in organic matter are buried by geological processes, fossil fuels or hydrocarbons are created. The pressure and heat of geological processes over millions of years transform the organic matter into such things as coal seams, and oil and gas reservoir rocks.

Technological advances in energy capture have transformed civilisation. Agriculture, the process of using plants to capture, in a manner of speaking, solar energy, was a key advance. Sailing ships to capture wind energy – which indirectly derives from the sun – was another key advance.

The advances which created our civilisation were the exploitation of fossil fuels – first coal in England in the 18th and 19th centuries, and then oil and gas in the 20th. You might say that the British Empire was built on sailing ships and then coal, and the American Empire was built on oil and gas. Oil fuels most of the world's transport by air, ship, truck and rail. Most electricity is generated using fossil fuels (coal and gas) to raise steam, which turns rotating equipment to 'agitate' the electrons.

So why are fossil fuels finite resources?

Fossil fuels can be thought of as a finite stock of 'ancient sunlight' trapped in chemical bonds in geologically altered hydrocarbons such as coal, oil and natural gas. They are finite because they were created over millions of years during geological history. At present rates of consumption, fossil fuels will be largely consumed over a few hundred years. Geological forces are not creating new fossil fuels at a rate that could conceivably replace stocks consumed. Fossil fuels cannot be replaced on any economic time horizon.

Renewable energy can be thought of as resulting from a flow of recent solar energy – like the hydrocarbons made by plants in agricultural activities.

What will happen when fossil fuels run out?

There is an interesting mix of physical, economic and political factors at work.

Will fossil fuels *physically* run out? There's a lot of hair splitting concerning the amount of the Oil Originally in Place (OOIP) in an oil reservoir rock and how much is extracted by oil wells. The most that is usually extracted is between 30% and 50% of the OOIP. New techniques like horizontal wells extract more oil. These issues are the deck chairs on the *Titanic*. Oil fields eventually run dry. Will it happen with one or a few massive discontinuities in supply? Possibly. For example, a huge proportion of Saudi oil derives from one giant field, Ghawar, and there is speculation about what its remaining life may be.

Most professional geologists who have studied the problem expect increases in global oil supplies to be very hard to achieve in the next few years and for supply to decline thereafter.

There are many responses to tighter supply from fewer oil fields. One is the search for substitutes. There are plentiful substitutes.

Natural gas is not in short supply and 'peak gas' is a long way off. Uranium is relatively plentiful and electricity from nuclear power stations is relatively inexpensive. The key problem with oil is that it is the main fuel for transport. Gas and uranium are not very good transport fuels.

The economic consequences of tight oil supply depend in large part on the *political* responses. One response is 'resource nationalism'. This involves supplier governments putting up prices by applying larger taxes. If global 'free trade' survives tighter oil supply then higher prices will to some extent 'ration out' the remaining oil. Resource nationalism will probably dictate that the domestic oil prices of producer countries will be below the level of international prices.

The single biggest economic response to tighter supply will be a higher oil price. In many places gas prices are contractually linked to oil prices and this link may break. The ramifications of higher oil prices are hard to overestimate!

So you believe in 'Peak Oil' theory?

The evidence is pretty compelling and corresponds with common sense. Oil fields decline. Charts of oil production in the USA for, say, Texas, Louisiana, Arkansas and so on show classic bell curves. The American geologist Hubbert predicted that supply from the lower 48 states would peak around 1975, and with hindsight we can see that that he was right. The same principles apply to global oil production. Oil is a fossil fuel that is just not being made by the natural ecosystem at anything remotely approaching a 'replacement' rate! Practically all the world's significant oil basins were discovered before 1930. New discoveries are in inaccessible places – for example, three kilometres below the seabed in water depths of two kilometres! Oil from these locations is expensive. And the risks are greater than society has generally acknowledged – as BP's now infamous Macondo well in the Gulf of Mexico showed.

Even large discoveries – say 25 billion barrels of OOIP – are small in relation to annual consumption, which is running at more than 30 billion barrels per annum.

And what about Global Warming?

Global temperatures have risen and are predicted to rise. The debate is about the causes. There has been a growing consensus that a key cause, if not *the* cause, is carbon emission derived from human civilisation.

Is human civilisation able to change the climate? The idea would have seemed fanciful to bygone generations. But satellite evidence for the change is pretty compelling.

Global Warming as a theory is harder to 'prove' than Peak Oil theory. Regardless of whether it can be proven to the nth degree, the principle that 'prevention is better than cure' is a good one in this case since, for much of the human race, there will be no cure.

The preventive measures put in place and in contemplation by government, particularly the European Union, envisage massive substitution of electricity generation equipment. The plan is to substitute coal- and gas-fired generation with 'green', wind and nuclear generation. If implemented, these plans require massive capital investment and imply higher electricity prices.

So what are the economic consequences of Peak Oil and Global Warming?

Serious! They imply the rebuilding of much of the energy infrastructure that supports our civilisation. A series of very big decisions need to be made at government and inter-governmental levels. The costs of the capital investments required will be enormous, and the costs of getting it wrong may be even greater.

One of the key challenges posed by Global Warming is that the costs of carbon emissions are not directly or immediately felt or borne by the emitter. The economic ecosystem has difficulty accounting for these sorts of costs. The stock of carbon dioxide has not been rigorously measured down the years. Since the stock crosses national frontiers, some internationally agreed methodology is required. There is also the difficulty of achieving agreement to control current 'flows' of carbon emissions without addressing the question of responsibility for the accumulated stock of carbon. To solve the problem, unprecedented political collaboration is needed. Will the politicians rise to the challenge?

You talk about the short term and the long term in resource economics. How do these differ?

Timescales differ in importance in different business models. In 'service' and 'distribution' business models the near term is critical. Capacity in service models may be ephemeral. A room night or a seat mile only exists for a particular time period and then disappears irretrievably. In distribution models, product is typically delivered over the short term – days and weeks, not months and years. Management in these businesses can afford to be blasé about capacity because it is often bought 'off the shelf' as a commodity.

In resources business models and also in capital goods business models it can take years and decades to develop new product or new capacity. Building a dam, a nuclear power station or a coal mine or developing an oil field requires concerted and prolonged effort.

Once built, these assets and the products they produce are often taken for granted. How much thought has gone into the consequences of the decline of North Sea oil production for the UK? It is possible that government simply believes that free trade will allow the importation of these resources.

What other business models are required by civilisation beyond finance and resources business models?

Capital goods business models

'Capital goods' are needed. Capital goods are things that are not consumed immediately, but endure over long periods, sometimes very long periods. 'Capital goods business models' design and build 'capital goods'.

If we think of a capital good as something which delivers a capability over a long period of time then many things fall into the definition. A capital good is not necessarily a machine like a car. Software programmes are capital goods which last for many years – sometimes decades, but more often five to seven years. One can think of human beings, for example, as capital goods. A doctor, a lawyer or a plumber is a capital good.

Capital goods make up much of the structure of modern civilisation. Public infrastructure projects such as roads, railways and ports are such large endeavours that they are often sponsored by the state. The State must finance the development of the capital goods required to wage war, armaments, because they are so specialised, their market so restricted and their production runs so short. 'Capital ships' like aircraft carriers are the embodiments of generations of technical expertise – and if they are sunk, the course of history is sometimes changed. Other capital goods are owned by citizens on average wages – consumer durables like washing machines, or motor cars. The roll-out of the motor car and domestic electricity over the last hundred years has profoundly changed civilisation in developed economies.

What is the *raison d'être* of capital goods?

A successful capital good delivers lasting productivity for its owner. It often makes it economic to do or make something which was not feasible at an affordable price before.

This applies to a simple 'consumer durable' such as a toaster, a kettle or a washing machine as much as to expensive and complex capital goods such as ports, jet airliners or oil tankers.

Hans Rosling, a professor at Sweden's Karolinska Institute, explains the transformative effects of the life-changing productivity benefits of apparently 'simple' capital goods that we take for granted, like a washing machine. At the end of a lecture on the benefits of washing machines he closes with the statements: 'Thank you, industrialisation. Thank you, steel mill. Thank you, power station and thank you, chemical processing industry that gave us time to read books!'[20]

What is distinctive about a capital goods business model?

As they become established, capital goods put down a 'footprint', an installed base of users. The installed base may be a 'parc' of cars, say the 2.1 cars per household in a saturated, developed car market. The installed base in its turn requires servicing to keep it running. Cars need Maintenance Repair Overhaul (MRO) services like replacement exhaust pipes and tyres, general servicing and fuel from roadside petrol stations. Upstream from the capital good assembly process there develops an entire supply chain of subsystems, components and raw materials.

Capital goods in many ways create the structure of a civilisation. What determines the relative wealth of one economy over another? Adam Smith puts it down to a variety of factors from the rule of law, to competition, to the 'invisible hand'. In many ways, capital goods are the strategic high ground in an economy. The human capital in an economy, itself a capital good, and the quantum, variety and productivity of other capital goods, together with the available natural resources, do much to create the standard of living. This is related to Keynes' macroeconomic insight that *the* critical step in the production

[20] www.gapminder.org/; www.ted.com

cycle is *investment*. Investment implies significant investment in capital goods – whether it be the education of physicists or nurses, or the update of a software programme or the next model of car or aircraft.

What determines demand for capital goods?

Several factors determine demand for capital goods – and usually combine to give it a pronounced cycle. Since capital goods are expensive and require significant financial capital to build and acquire, the credit cycle is often the most important determinant of demand. Demand for capital goods is also greatly influenced by their productivity, which in turn is determined by the rate of technological progress. The rate of adoption of a capital good is determined by the degree to which the target market is 'saturated'. Adoption rates tend to follow an S-curve – slow at first, as a market first adopts a new product, then rapid as the market is penetrated, and then slow once the market is saturated.

Are capital goods business models riskier than most?

All the archetypal business models have specific risks associated with them. The key risk with capital goods businesses is the size and evolution of their installed base of products and customers. The installed base in turn is a major determinant of the service revenues that the business receives. Service revenues tend to recur over the life of the capital good and are generally less risky than the 'original equipment' sale.

The growth path for an installed base typically follows an S pattern. At the bottom of the S-curve capital goods projects face a multitude of huge challenges. A product has to be made, often with an untried technology, and demonstrated. The customer must be persuaded of the productivity benefits – which may only flow if the customer re-engineers its processes to accommodate the new product. Often finance must be provided for the customer. The product must be perfected, the production process accelerated. All the while the clock is ticking. Will the financial capital to finance the development losses run out before volume sales are achieved, unit costs fall and the positive feedback loop from lower prices to higher sales kicks in?

The middle of the S-curve is a sweet spot for investors where value is created and realised by rapid customer adoption of the product. Once the installed base reaches a critical mass and a steady adoption rate is achieved, all sorts of economies of scale kick in.

At the top of the S-curve the installed base stops growing and then goes into decline. If the product is superseded by a new technology which is more efficient, the rate of decline can be precipitous.

In a developed country capital goods are all around: the pavements under one's feet, the power cables overhead, the mobile phone in one's hand, the cars, trains and buses one steps into. They make life so easy! And yet capital goods business models are among the most difficult to create and operate. Getting a new capital good adopted by a market is in many ways a heroic endeavour which invariably costs more money, takes longer and requires greater endurance than is ever anticipated at the start.

Are capital goods just physical products?

A capital good is a product that endures across time and creates productivity benefits. So computer software is a capital good as much as a ditch or a road or a machine. Trained people can be thought of as capital goods too. The growth of the installed base of trained people in professions tends to follow an S-curve in similar fashion to the installed base of cars or airliners.

Risky, but rewarding! What other generic business models can we invest in?

Once the capital goods are built, service business models are needed to operate the capital goods.

Services business models

Services are said to be the biggest bit of the economy. What's 'archetypal' about service business models?

Service businesses *operate* things rather than make them. When people think of services, they often think of services supplied by people – things like haircuts supplied by hairdressers. Services span an enormous range of activities from accounting services to maintenance repair and overhaul of jet engines. The common feature of services business models is that they operate an installed base of capital goods.

A hairdresser does not sound like an installed base of capital goods!

The reason is that one single hairdresser is implicitly a 'sole trader'; in other words, a very small installed base. And the capital good which is operated by the hairdresser is him- or herself. If one accepts that the training invested in acquiring the hairdressing skills represents a form of capital good, one can see that even a sole trader offering a specialised skill which takes time and money to acquire is operating a capital good.

So what does this vast variety of service businesses have in common?

The common thing is the management of the installed base of capital goods. Getting a return out of an installed base is about managing capacity utilisation and achieved price or yield. That's the same whether the capital good is a hotel, a civil airliner, an accounting firm or a chain of hairdressing shops. The key issues are capacity and the return on the capacity. So hotel management looks at Revenue per Available Room (Revpar), an airline looks at Revenue per Available Seat Mile (RASM), an accounting firm looks at revenue per billable hour and a hairdressing chain looks at revenue per available hairdresser. The minutiae of each service business is different, but the capacity utilisation problem is similar. The problem is to keep utilisation high while maintaining a product mix that achieves a good average price.

How do service businesses maintain high utilisation and yield?

There are many ways – most of which are specific to the business. Customer service and marketing are important. Specialisation is important. Share of capacity and capacity utilisation and pricing is seldom uniform across all the players in an industry. Most service businesses will achieve below industry average utilisation and pricing. This is because their industries are very competitive and the product is not differentiated. Most service businesses go through capacity cycles. The margins of companies in the same service industry tend to go up together. This in turn leads the industry as a whole to order new capacity. Over-capacity leads to a fall in profitability.

What is the next archetypal business model?

Distribution business models

Distribution. Distributing product is essential to modern civilisation. Production is centralised to achieve economies of scale in manufacture or product creation. Once created, product must be distributed. Most distribution is time critical.

What's special about distribution businesses?

Network effects. Distribution businesses tend to be or have the potential to become 'natural monopolies'. The reason for this is that as the network gets bigger the average costs of supplying the users fall. The incremental customer costs little to bolt on. The technical definition of a 'natural monopoly' is a business where the average cost curve slopes downwards – in other words, the marginal costs of the incremental customers are lower than the average cost. Some capital goods and process businesses may benefit from first mover advantages or unique patents or know-how, but they don't usually enjoy the same network effects.

Monopolies give good returns! Why wouldn't we just own distribution businesses then?

One reason is that the monopoly characteristics in some of these businesses are obvious and government therefore regulates the returns that they are allowed to make. This is the case with most so-called 'utility' businesses. Distributors of natural resources – water or gas or electricity networks – and distributors of information, analogue waves and digital 'bits and bytes' have many the features of natural monopolies. If they were unregulated, these businesses would have the power to push up prices and make super normal profits.

Government has addressed this problem in many ways. The first way was simply to nationalise these businesses. This, of course, does not solve the problem – which is that consumers get a bad deal and the companies have no incentives to improve; it simply means that the profits go to the State (and management and employees).

The next way around is to introduce regulation. In practice, many different regulatory systems exist and they vary in sophistication. Some systems define the Regulated Asset Base and prescribe the rate of return that can be earned on it. In other systems the regulator effectively does a cash-flow forecast, taking into account the capex (capital expenditure) and opex (operating expenditure) and required efficiency savings, and allows prices to increase by just enough to allow the companies to make an internal rate of return on the cash invested of something a bit greater than the 'risk-free rate' on government bonds. The companies sit down with the regulator at each review – typically every five years – and debate the inputs. The companies set out their capex, opex and savings plans. The regulator then allows price increases which will provide a given rate of return, provided the companies deliver on their forecasts. This gives the companies an incentive to become more efficient.

Can't we find unregulated distribution businesses?

Yes, we can. The regulation that investors are most wary of is profits regulation, because this may cap the potential investment upside. Most businesses are regulated in some manner though. There are many forms of 'distribution' business. These include intermediary businesses like insurance brokers distributing insurance, or estate agents 'distributing' housing information. Television stations are distributors of content; supermarkets are distributors of food.

Distribution seems to cover a very wide variety of products.

In a developed economy that uses capital goods, production and processing are centralised to achieve economies of scale and the product is then distributed. In subsistence economies everything is done locally – but the standard of living is not often very high.

Not many real world business models are pure versions of the archetypal versions. Most are an amalgam of several archetypes and could be categorised in more than one 'bucket'. Supermarkets are a case in point. A supermarket chain can be put into a distribution bucket because it buys wholesale and sells retail and the logistics of moving the goods, the distribution, is a significant part of the business. But it is also a 'service' business, servicing an installed base of supermarkets and the capacity utilisation of the floor space, measured by sales per square foot, is also critical. The profits of supermarkets are not regulated, although many other aspects are, because competition between supermarket chains generally keeps them 'honest'. Supermarkets do have some monopolistic elements – but these are more related to the real estate they use. Real estate planning rules regulate the building of supermarkets. The difficulties of getting planning permission for a supermarket constitute a barrier to entry for competition. And once a supermarket is established in a certain area, most people in its 'catchment area' will tend to use it because of its physical location.

Are there any other archetypal business models?

Yes there are two others: process business models and intellectual property business models.

Process business models

What's archetypal about process business models?

All businesses are collections of processes. In process business models the business is effectively the process. In process business models there's one key process around which the business is built. So a smelting business takes raw materials, puts them through a process and produces metal. A data processing business takes data, say payroll data, and uses it to produce payslips. An oil refinery takes crude oil and cracks it into a range of different sorts of molecule.

What determines which processes are inside and which outside the business organisation?

Whether a process becomes a business depends in large part on the 'minimum efficient scale' (MES) of the process. If the MES is small then everyone performs the process for themselves. They don't have to buy it from a business. Once personal computers made computing power affordable, most businesses bought PCs and networks and performed much of their own data processing. When computing power was expensive the MES of a computer system was very large, and so smaller businesses subcontracted their data processing to third party specialist data processors.

Not many mines would contemplate owning a smelter because the MES is very large and requires inputs from many mines to achieve effective capacity utilisation.

So technology seems to be very important in process business models?

Yes, in several different ways. The technology creates the process. The creation of a new capital good can create a new process. Competitive advantage in processing businesses can revolve around whether access to the technology is exclusive. When Arkwright first patented his cotton spinning machine he had exclusive use of it. Subsequently, England became the cotton spinning centre for the whole world. Later still, the process has been taken to low wage economies like China.

Arguably technology creates processes, which 'create' civilisation.

What do you mean by that?

In a Communist utopia all the means of production are melded together into one giant organisation owned by the State, and resources are allocated across the activities according to a 'central plan'. In a pre-industrial utopia individual households control all their own means of production, living on self-sufficient 'homesteads' or small farms. These utopian structures have been very difficult to create in the 'real' world and when implemented have turned into dystopias.

Why don't they work?

Because the technology required for completely centralised production or completely distributed production is not very effective. The ideas are not utterly impossible to implement, the technology just does not exist to enable them to work at all efficiently. Technology in this sense includes legal and accounting technology as well as engineering technology. At present, it just does not make sense for every household to generate their own electricity. A coal-fired power station is just much more efficient but has very large MES. But the electricity generation process is not fixed in stone for all time. New ways of doing things are discovered – solar power, energy stored in the form of hydrogen derived from electrolysis of water and so on. These things might one day change the shape of civilisation.

Intellectual property business models

Do intellectual property business models have the potential to change civilisation?

Yes, in theory. In practice the pure IP model, as opposed to the business and know-how built around it, does not often represent good 'economic value'.

Why is that?

To explain what I mean I have to define 'intellectual property' or IP. IP is a legally created monopoly, a monopoly that the state grants to a company or person. The state has its motives. *Raison d'etat!* The State usually gives these sorts of privileges if it perceives that society will get a commensurate or greater benefit. This alone should put us on notice. There's no such thing as a free lunch, and 'free monopolies' are usually 'free' for a reason – the reason being that they are not at first worth very much.

What sorts of legal monopoly does the State grant?

They fall into a few main categories. One is patents. These create a 20-year monopoly, provided it can be shown that the idea is new and original. Another is an 'exploration and production licence' or EPL, which gives exclusive rights to minerals discovered in a defined geographical area – say, oil and gas or copper and gold. Another is copyright, exclusive rights to original published works – say a novel or a software programme.

So why aren't these sorts of legal monopolies worth a great deal?

Paradoxically IP in and of itself is not worth very much. It can be a key. But it's not worth much without the roller-skates! What creates the economic value is all the work that goes into building a business with its associated profits around the IP. A time limited monopoly of some IP by itself without the associated business know-how, processes and customers may not have much economic value.

Clearly the IP is worth something. But how much? It is necessary to identify the source of the economic value; that is, the cash surpluses which will derive from the IP. The value of pure IP, say a patented idea, without a developed product, customers and business model is an option value. It may be worth a little or a lot. Much of the value is given to the option by the determination and depth of pockets of the financial backers who 'make it happen'.

Are IP businesses big business then?

Yes and no.

It is worth distinguishing between a pure archetypal IP business and businesses which use IP. *All* businesses use know-how or IP which is not legally protected to the same extent. Many businesses own clearly identifiable IP. But most businesses are better categorised in some other archetypal business model. Resources companies own IP, but the special features of resources economics capture more of the features of their businesses than the IP which they own. There's a market for buying into oil and gas projects – 'farming-in'. But the IP is not very valuable to anyone who does not already have the infrastructure to exploit it. Pharmaceutical companies own patented drugs. Sometimes it is the molecule or the biological agent which is patented, sometimes the use to which it is put, sometimes the manner of making the molecule. The patents represent barriers to entry. But the economics of distribution business models does more to explain the profitability of pharma companies than the patents.

So do pure IP businesses exist?

Yes, and they are a comparatively recent phenomenon. An 'industry' has also developed to take pure IP from universities and to develop businesses around the IP. This is particularly common in the drug industry, where early stage 'biotech' businesses seek to develop new drugs.

So do pure IP businesses have a lot of economic value?

They have the potential to create economic value. But they don't usually have positive cashflows or balance sheets. So all the economic value lies somewhere in the future. As a result, the economic value is particularly subjective and risky. The commercialisation of pure IP has great *social* value but little immediate economic value. A portfolio of projects to commercialise pure IP will have a wide range of results from complete failure to great success. Picking the projects that will be winners at such an early stage is especially difficult. The near-term economic value is for the intermediaries who promote the sale of the shares and for the management who get a free option on developing a business.

You have described seven archetypal 'business models'.
Are any of them intrinsically better investments? What makes
a business model intrinsically better?

There are several factors: reliability or predictability of cash
surpluses, ease of understanding, duration of projects and
cashflows, and type of risk exposure.

'Predictability' and 'understandability' sound easy enough. In
fact, they are hard. Knowing what you need to understand in
order to understand is one issue. Understanding that you don't
understand is another. One of the main reasons why Warren
Buffett[21] has been so successful is that he stays within his area of
competence. Most people are seduced by novelty or intellectual
curiosity or silken-tongued salesmanship.

The predictability and duration of cashflows in different
business models tends to differ. Capital goods and lending
businesses, particularly when they are relatively immature,
are difficult to predict. On the other hand, to the extent it
is possible to generalise, services and distribution businesses
are relatively easier to predict and their cashflows are often
repeatable for longer.

Business models can be thought of as 'objective' – stuff that
is 'auditable'. Much of investment is subjective – in the heads
of investors. In theory, at the right price *any* business could
be an investment.

So what is the 'right price'?

The 'right price' is where the value received is at least as large
as the price paid. We talked a lot about 'fundamental analysis'
– the investigation of what the value might be. We have not

---

[21] Warren Buffett is an American investor, industrialist and philanthropist. He is
widely regarded as one of the most successful investors in the world.

talked about how prices are determined. Price is whatever the investors want to pay. In much of economic theory, the way in which prices are created was a question which was sort of 'shelved' by assuming that 'normally' investors would a) act in their own self-interest and b) act in an economically 'rational' manner. More recently, 'behavioural economics' has sought to discover just how realistic these assumptions are.

In investment the examination of prices for their own sake is the subject of so-called 'technical analysis'.

CHAPTER   8

Technical analysis

'Where fundamental analysis focuses on value, technical analysis concerns itself with price, volume of transactions and individual/group psychology.'

– **Bronwin Wood,** *Society of Technical Analysts*

What's 'technical analysis'?

Fundamental analysis looks at value and technical analysis looks at prices, particularly prices presented in graphical or chart format. Price is what someone will pay, which is subjective and varies from person to person. Value in investment jargon is 'economic value', an estimate of the present value of future cash surpluses that the underlying business models are expected to produce. Value is not an entirely objective thing either. It becomes less certain and therefore less objective the further out in time it lies. But there are facts and principles around which to debate objective values. As we've discussed, price and value have an uneasy relationship. What someone will pay may be an economically 'rational' choice and it may also be greatly influenced by perception – and hence psychology.

What do we get out of technical analysis?

Price is subjective. Technical analysis provides some insight into the subjective factors that affect price. When shown in chart format, a huge quantity of price data over many years can be condensed into a few lines on a graph. This summarises the historical record of what investors actually did – in terms of the prices and quantities of stock that they traded. The resulting information is not scientific, in the sense of being susceptible to analysis which can give predictions of future results with near certainty. But it can be used to make inferences about the opinion and psychology of investors.

Does it work?

Opinion about technical analysis can be polarised. Some people swear by it and never look at fundamentals. Others believe that price data alone has no predictive value. Indeed, it can be shown that a random number generator will also produce price patterns which chartists consider significant – such as a 'head and shoulders' pattern.

One way of looking at technical analysis is to think of it as the history of a particular price. Just as history does not have the power to predict the future, price charts cannot make fail-safe predictions. But statements about the future are also statements about the past. Past and future form part of a continuum. So it is wrong to say that charts have no value. Patterns clearly repeat. Prices which rise rapidly or go exponential usually come back down. Most prices have some mean reverting tendency. The mean varies over time depending on both fundamentals and on perception. The mean to which prices revert tends to be some core economic value.

Taken out of context or in isolation, technical analysis can be so much voodoo. But taken in conjunction with knowledge of the fundamentals, technical analysis provides some insight into investor psychology. For example, it is said that share prices 'walk up the steps and come down in the lift'. This is a common phenomenon at the level of the market as a whole, for whole sectors and for individual stocks. Technical analysis by itself cannot predict these patterns with certainty. But a rising trend can represent a growing consensus of opinion about the profit prospects for a particular company or sector and therefore be a reflection of investor perception and psychology.

So how much weight should you give technical analysis?

Equities don't usually pay big dividends and they seldom liquidate themselves to return the capital invested. So the return made depends on buying and selling in the market. Technical analysis therefore has to be a significant factor.

There are only two ways of making a return from owning equities. One is the fundamental cash surpluses which the underlying business model makes from supplying a product to customers – reflected in profits and ultimately in dividends.

The other is the return 'made from the market'. This can be thought of politely as the return from assuming 'risk' and impolitely as the return made out of other investors. Making money by creating some capability to satisfy a customer at a profit is a 'win–win' proposition rather than a zero-sum game. More customers buying more product creates more 'added value' and all the 'stakeholders' in the business benefit. Making money out of other investors is a zero-sum game – where one person's gain is equivalent to another person's loss.

How do you make money out of other investors?

Well, there are legal and illegal ways of making money out of other investors. An illegal way would be by trading on the back of the certain knowledge of price-sensitive facts which are not available to all investors – insider dealing. For most of economic history, insider dealing was not illegal. For example, one reason that non-executive directors did not receive a significant salary in some businesses (like the Bank of England!) was that it was considered that the information they were privy to had a value in its own right.

Another illegal way of making money out of other investors is for a majority shareholder to 'oppress' minority shareholders. This has been a sufficiently common practice for English law to have built up a significant case history of precedents. What exactly constitutes 'oppression' can be difficult to define, and there's plenty of scope for gamesmanship and sharp practice.

So what are the legal ways of making money out of other investors?

A legal way of making money out of other investors is to arbitrage human frailty – psychology. This has been succinctly described as 'being brave when others are fearful and fearful when others are brave'. This is a risky activity. Prices that drop 90% may drop another 90% and shares that double in value may double again.

Do you have any qualms about exploiting 'human frailty'?

Well, yes and no.

A market simply facilitates human action. It accepts a plurality of different opinions about the world, whilst enforcing strict rules about how those opinions are expressed by trading on the market.

Everyone is different and is entitled to their own opinion. At a temporal level, everyone touches reality at different points from different places. Individuals have different perspectives on time. Ten days or a month may be a long time for one investor, five years for another and twenty-five years for another. Investors also differ in industriousness, levels of knowledge and perceptions of risk. An investor may have 10% of a very risky capital goods company. For someone in one set of circumstances, the investment might be extremely rash.

For someone in another, it might be a calculated risk. Much depends on the price paid.

A market does not seek to prescribe opinion or tell people what to think. Differences in the perceptions of individual investors are impossible to perceive from the outside. A market has to allow the participants the freedom to participate and it must oblige them to take responsibility for their actions. Markets prescribe some 'norms' that should be maintained. Many of these norms are enforced with formidable discipline – such as settlement rules. Others norms are policed although they are more difficult to enforce, like insider trading rules. Provided investors satisfy the basic rules for participating in a market and the market enforces the rules fairly then all the participants can be taken to be 'consenting adults'. Each participant must take responsibility for their own actions.

In the nature of things some participants will do some silly things some of the time. Occasionally the entire market may be gripped by belief in something – like the power of the internet or the 'digital economy' – and in its enthusiasm 'over-anticipate' the future; in other words, pay too much. Both silly and sensible things get done on markets.

An idealist might wish that all investors were equally industrious, rational and judicious in weighing the odds. But utopian ideals have difficulty coping with human freedom and responsibility. Part of freedom is the freedom to make mistakes, and failure is part of the price of freedom.

An idealist might argue that an investor who buys shares after they have fallen 50% has 'exploited' the seller. But the buyer does not normally know who the seller is. The seller might be making a profit by selling, even after a sharp fall in price. The buyer can equally be seen as offering the seller a service – the provision of liquidity. Any subsequent profit can be seen as a reward for putting hard-earned capital at risk.

So the market is efficient then?

We have to be very careful what we mean by 'efficient'.

There has been a lot of academic research into the 'efficiency' of markets. But efficiency as defined in these studies is quite a special thing. The academic research really seeks to test whether markets can be consistently beaten – whether or not there are simple rules or algorithms which can be applied to do consistently better than the market average return.

These tests do indeed show that the market is difficult to beat. But this is not much different from saying that it is difficult consistently to take money off bookmakers; very difficult.

It is a mistake to go from these tests of efficiency to the conclusion that markets are 'perfect', that it is not possible to do better or worse than the market. The market return for this purpose is itself an artificial construct. It is an average of the returns from a concocted basket of stocks that are deemed to be 'representative' of the market as a whole.

The fact that properly functioning markets are 'fair' in their own terms does not mean that we have to accept that the market is the only reality, or to believe that markets are 'perfect'. There is a great deal about markets that is very imperfect. Markets share some characteristics with casinos. Some people lose and some people 'make' a lot of money in remarkably short spaces of time – just as some punters in casinos make and lose a lot of money. Markets can be extremely dangerous.

Perception of markets swings like a pendulum. In the 1930s 'capitalism' was widely perceived to have failed. Mass unemployment caused great suffering. Social commentators like George Orwell were critical of the 'system' and advocated forms of communism as a solution. In the 1980s the pendulum swung the other way and markets were considered a panacea.

Although at a temporal level everyone touches reality at different points, at a spiritual level there is still the intuition that everyone touches reality at the same point – a mystery for which the one-word summary, 'God', is too brief to explain.

The truth is paradoxical. The 'efficient markets hypothesis' is a theory which can be tested and 'proven' at one level, and at another level it is an extremely dangerous notion!

How does psychology affect share price volatility?

Market capitalisations are volatile. They can vary by plus or minus 25% a year, or more. There are good reasons for much of the volatility. Equity in businesses which have borrowed significantly, or which own difficult to value options, or which have high fixed costs and volatile end demand will fluctuate in value.

Do market capitalisations vary more than a best estimate of the present value of the future cash surpluses?

Yes, they probably do. The explanation for this is human psychology.

Why is that?

Suppose you asked ten people to estimate the life expectancy of, say, the president of Germania. 'Objective' approaches to giving an answer would consider the person's age, family history and lifestyle. An answer based on statistical analysis of thousands of comparable lives could be prepared. Suppose the 'objective' answer is 20 years.

If the same people were polled once a month for twenty-four months it is quite likely that they would change their estimates from one month to the next. Statistical life expectancy does not change very much over two years. But the people polled might well be swayed by recent events. They might become more optimistic if they saw the president playing golf and more pessimistic if there were a national flu epidemic. Fine tuning the predicted life expectancy of the president based on recent experience may not be completely irrational – but it may not result in a more accurate estimate either.

'Behavioural economics' tests people's decisions under conditions of uncertainty and discovers, unsurprisingly, that most people are not dispassionate like Mr Spock in *Star Trek*. People dislike taking losses, they are more inclined to take risks to recover losses, and prefer to 'not lose money' than to make it. We all have a natural tendency to do today what we should have done yesterday – even if it is too late because the price has moved.

Human nature has not changed much over thousands of years. It comes down to fear and greed. Fear is provoked by things like unexpected changes of management, restatement of accounting figures, loss of contracts, acts of God like fires. Greed is provoked by seeing another piece of good news, things like a new contract win, a new mineralised intersection or a new product launch.

A well-known internet retail business called ASOS had its warehouse next door to an oil storage depot in North London called Buncefield. When the depot exploded, its warehouse was destroyed. The share price fell immediately by 30% and then fell more despite the fact that the loss was fully insured. Across the market random events like this are regular occurrences. When market makers and buyers withdraw, it creates a hiatus in the price. And the lower price serves to deter nervous sellers.

Most share prices are far more volatile than the fortunes of the underlying businesses. The different amplitude of share price swings in relation to realistic changes in overall cash generation of the business can be loosely explained by a combination of changes in investor psychology and in overall liquidity in the financial system.

And how does overall bank credit affect price volatility?

Bank credit and money are created simultaneously. The money is spent. Some of the money finds its way into financial assets, pushing up their prices. When the price of an equity share rises, implicitly the duration of its expected cash surpluses also rises. From one perspective this can be thought of as an increase in optimism – because prices are implicitly looking out further into the future. From another perspective the higher prices result from the cycle of growth and contraction of bank credit.

You've talked about 'economic value' or 'fundamentals', which can be estimated to within a broad or narrow tolerance. You've talked about how prices are subjective but can be studied using 'technical analysis'. Neither 'value' nor 'price' are certain. How do you think about 'risk'?

Different people define risk in different ways. A statistician uses statistical rules to make predictions and to work out the probability of certain things happening. One definition of risk is that 'more things can happen than will happen'. In other words, the events which actually take place are a subset of all the possible events.

Objectivity

CHAPTER 9

Risk

> *'If we want to achieve something, we have to be willing to take risks.'*
>
> – Benjamin Franklin

What is your definition of risk?

In investment, risk is the difference between price and value.

Risk is low when price and value are close to each other or when value exceeds price. Risk is great when value and price have the potential to diverge significantly.

Risk is usually taken to mean downside risk, risk of loss. If value exceeds price, there's risk on the upside. But, of course, it all depends where you are starting from. If you are short a share then it is less risky if you believe price exceeds value.

In relation to a business, value means economic value, in other words the present value of the future cash surpluses it will produce, and price means the market value of all the claims on those cashflows.

Risk is difficult to assess for many reasons. One elementary reason is that some people may not be using the same definitions of price and value. For example, if you do not accept that a pension scheme deficit is a claim on the future cashflows of the company, you will arrive at a different view of the price you are paying. Similarly, if you think you are making a 'social' investment which has non-cash benefits by improving 'quality of life', you may perceive more value than someone who is just looking dispassionately at the cash surplus generation potential.

Even supposing we are all using the same definitions, risk is difficult to assess because price and value vary over time. In theory price is supposed, ultimately, to be derived from value. The difficulty is the word 'ultimately' – because this implies that, given enough time, price will converge on value. In practice, price can move independently of value for long periods of time and vice versa. As Keynes said, the market can remain irrational for longer than you can remain solvent.

How does this compare with a statistical view of risk?

Mathematicians have discovered some very valuable statistical 'laws' or rules. These rules allow us to look at data and work out its statistical characteristics – such as what the average piece of data is, what the standard deviation is and so on. These rules allow us to make inferences about individual items of data and estimate the likelihood or risk that they belong to a particular data set. If the average height of men were five feet ten inches and if the standard deviation were one foot, then statistical science would tell you that a nine-foot man was extremely unlikely.

Can statistics tell you if something is cheap or expensive?

For some things it can and for some it can't. For a simple commodity product, say a can of baked beans, statistical analysis of prices of baked beans over time will probably give a reliable guide to when baked beans are good value and when bad value.

This sort of statistical analysis works well for things which do not vary much with time. Baked beans were probably pretty similar 50 years ago to what they are today. Experiments in physics are often time-independent. The nature of physical forces like electricity or gravity does not change perceptibly over time.

For data populations whose characteristics change over time, statistical analysis is more complicated and has to allow for this. The average height of men has changed over time. But the change has been slow and analysis can compensate for this.

For a characteristic like the value of an individual business, statistical analysis is complicated by the fact that the social value of a business is a matter of judgement, even taste; the accounting value is a matter of judgement; and the economic value, including future cashflows, is especially subjective.

The average height of men is objective and changes slowly over time. The economic value of a business is subjective and may change very rapidly. The cash surpluses which are taken into the economic value and the rate at which they are discounted are both subjective. It is as if we were trying to estimate the average height of a species over its entire life before it becomes extinct. To do this we have to estimate whether and when it may become extinct and bring into account the average height pertaining to the future life of the species as well as the average height that pertained in the past.

If we were trying to ascertain the average height of a population, rather than its average economic value, our sample of measurements would be objective. The measuring device would be accurate to a fine tolerance. With economic value the measuring device is a market – comprising individuals operating under different assumptions and incentives. So the data is being measured at any given time using different measuring devices, and over time the people doing the measuring and their measuring devices change.

The data available to measure economic value is market price data. Price data is 'meta data' rather than data itself; it is a subjective opinion expressed at a point in time about the data rather than the data itself.

So you are saying that market price data is different in type from data about physical properties like height or weight?

Yes. It is a phenomenon which statisticians call 'stationarity'. A distribution of outcomes of a stationary process remains the same, regardless of time or place. Many physical objects have this feature. The mass of a bar of gold is the same today as it was when Julius Caesar was alive, and is the same at the Antarctic as at the Equator. The value of an oil company is not stationary in a statistical sense. New discoveries, dry holes, capital raisings, new farm-in partners or new management can all have a dramatic effect on the valuation.

So should we use statistics?

Definitely, for many good reasons. One reason is that, ultimately, market price data does have to converge with cash data. Cash is the ultimate test of economic value. So the cash put into a business, the dividends taken out and the liquidation proceeds are indeed an 'objective' measure of economic value. One difficulty with the cash measure is that the value of cash itself changes over time. But this can be adjusted for. The main difficulty is that cash measures are only objective *ex post* – so the animal must be killed for the autopsy to be possible. 'Killing the animal', in a manner of speaking, actually does not present a problem for statisticians. They simply wait a long time. If the data is collected over a sufficiently long time, say 50 years, it becomes more and more objective and more like the problem of the average height of a population of human beings.

Doesn't that mean that statistical analysis works better for some problems than for others?

Yes, I think it does. Statistics work better for the market as a whole than for individual share prices. One reason for this is a statistical law called the Central Limit Theorem. This says that if you take several randomly distributed variables – like, say, the time series for the prices of many different shares – then the distribution of the sum or average of the different variables (prices) will tend to be normal. Theories to explain market returns like the Capital Asset Pricing Model depend on market returns being normally or log normally distributed.[22]

Are statistics useful for picking stocks?

If you are mainly interested in the difference between price and value then statistical mean variance analysis is not your main concern. A statistician would say you were more interested in the dispersion of the possible outcomes. A stock picker thinks that he can pick stocks where the dispersion of the possible returns is skewed in his favour. Achieving this sort of favourable skew is much easier with regard to things which exist in the present than with regard to things which may or may not happen in the future. A business which has substantial positive net assets and no debt, which is cash generative and which has a proven business model is less likely to become insolvent than a start-up with no net worth, no borrowings, no cash generation and an unproven business model. Simply because the second business is not self-financing, one of the possible outcomes must be insolvency. The dispersion of likely outcomes for the first business is positively skewed relative to the likely outcomes for

---

[22] The CAPM only works if the distribution of stockmarket returns is 'normal'. In other words the distribution must have the classic Gaussian bell shape with as many observations above the mean as below. Empirically the distribution is in fact skewed with a longer 'tail' of returns above the mean than below. However, when the log of the returns is taken the curve is approximately normal or bell shaped.

the second business. Someone promoting the second business will probably have a great story which leads one to suppose that the business has a net present value substantially greater than the price being proposed. Of course, the probabilities are subjective, but they are based on lots of experience of listening to business managers and promoters.

So how useful is mean variance analysis to stockpickers?

Mean variance analysis is useful in studying the possible paths along which share prices might travel. Dispersion and volatility are not unrelated. A wider range of possible outcomes creates the potential for more volatility. Some value investors adopt a stoic attitude to price volatility. Warren Buffett refers to it as 'quotational' risk, the risk of price quote offered by the manic-depressive Mr Market. Value investors 'sleep well at night' even if prices collapse, sure in the conviction that value is greater than price. Such a brave approach is easier when managing one's own money or in a closed end fund where the investors cannot demand their money back. Mutual fund managers cannot afford to be indifferent to 'quotational' risk because the investors can recall their money on demand and may be more inclined to ask for their money after a price decline than after a price rise.

How subjective is mean variance analysis?

Statistical techniques like mean variance analysis have the appearance of objectivity. My colleagues who understand statistics much better than I ever will say that there's a schism amongst statisticians between 'Frequentists' and 'Bayesians'. A crude caricature would describe Frequentists as believing that statistics are objective, and Bayesians as believing they are subjective.[23]

---

[23] *The Dawning of the Age of Stochasticity* by David Mumford is a brilliant exposition of the case for statistical reasoning.

Bayesians see every statistical analysis as based on some subjective a priori hypothesis. Bayesian inference can be amazingly powerful. It is used, for example, to de-convolute blurred images using the a priori hypothesis of 'maximum entropy', meaning that the most likely 'value' of any pixel is an average of the nearest pixels. The results are astonishing.[24] In the stock market a software company using Bayesian inference techniques to search databases has become a FTSE 100 company[25] within a decade of being founded.

So the usefulness of statistics reflects the inferences behind them!

Yes. An apparently logical inference is that price data for a given business over time reflects changes in the 'fundamentals' in the business. Something close to a 'law' in investment is that rising share prices correlate with rising earnings, for example. And yet other inferences such as the inference that prices are driven by the credit cycle, or that earnings and prices mean revert may have as much explanatory power as earnings.

The interest of statistical analysis of share prices is that it is an inference about data which is itself an inference about the fundamentals. The prices themselves shape the fundamentals. Statistical analysis of individual stock prices is still valuable. It tells you as much about how opinions or expectations about a stock are evolving as about the underlying 'platonic economic value'. So it can identify market 'enthusiasm' and 'boredom' with individual stocks. One reason for using some statistical analysis, which is an ironically good one, is simply that so many other investors are also using this analysis.

---

[24] www.maxent.co.uk gives some good examples.

[25] Autonomy Corporation PLC; www.autonomy.com

Do great investors use statistics?

They all use numbers. What they add to the numbers is meaning gained from experience. A visceral description of risk as a matter of consequences is found in one of the funniest and truest books ever written about the market, *Where Are the Customer's Yachts?* by Fred Schwed:

> *'Like all of Life's rich emotional experiences, the full flavour of losing important money cannot be conveyed by literature. Art cannot convey to an inexperienced girl what it is truly like to be a wife and mother. There are certain things which cannot be adequately explained to a virgin either by words or pictures. Nor can any description I might offer here even approximate to what it feels like to lose a real chunk of money that you used to own.'*

So give me an example of a low-risk asset.

Cash is a low-risk asset because its price and value coincide in the short term. Paradox may apply. Cash may not have any risk in the short term. But holding cash for decades can make you poorer if there is inflation, which reduces the real value of cash. Inflation has been the 'usual' state of affairs in developed economies. But as Japan's experience shows and as historical experience in the 1930s and before also show, deflation can also persist for long periods.

For some assets price is defined in terms of a value. So a mutual fund or unit trust publishes a net asset value every day. The net asset value of a mutual fund is the weighted average market price of the financial assets that it owns. The price at which a mutual fund is sold is, essentially, its net asset value. Prima facie it appears as if the price and value of a unit trust cannot differ. But of course, this is an illusion because the definition of value in this example is the 'market value' of the financial assets.

The market value is just a collection of prices which can differ from the underlying economic value of the different assets.

And a high-risk asset?

An equity share is a high-risk asset because the subjective elements in both the price and the value can be very large and consequently price and value can diverge by large amounts for long periods.
The price and value of a bond should not vary by as much as the price and value of an equity share, because the cash which derives from a bond is all defined upfront and is therefore known. The main risk with a bond is whether the issuer will perform on its obligations, not what the amount of the cash surpluses will be. Since a bond is 'self-liquidating' there's a fixed period of time before price has to converge with value.

So how do we work out what the risk is?

By thinking about probabilities. Thinking 'quantitatively' about probabilities does not come naturally to many people. But there's an entire branch of mathematics devoted to probability theory, which I probably would not understand and certainly cannot explain.

But let me try to explain probabilities at a very elementary level using horse racing as the example. Suppose there are 40 horses in a race, say the Grand National. If they all had an equal chance of winning, the probability of any one of them coming first would be 1 in 40 or, in bookmakers' terms, odds of 39 to 1.

The 'price' of a bet on one horse in the race might be odds of 39 to 1. How risky is that price? It all depends on what the 'real' chances of that horse winning are. The 'real' odds of the horse winning might be 1,000 to 1, in which case the bet at 39 to 1 is very risky because price is much greater than value. Or the 'real' odds of that horse winning may be 6 to 1 'on', meaning that you put down 6 in order to win 7 back, which is only a 'fair' bet if the horse is likely to win 85% of the time. If we can buy a bet for this horse to win at 39 to 1, implying a one in 40 chance of winning when the 'real' chance is 85%, then the risk is in our favour.

How do we know what the real chances of the horse winning are?

Some things are more knowable than others. Flat races are more predictable than races with fences. Fences introduce a big element of uncertainty. For example, the best horse in the race might be brought down at a fence by a mistake by the worst horse. This question of 'knowability' is sort of the difference between 'risk' and 'uncertainty'.

What's the difference between risk and uncertainty?

This is not so easy to explain, but I'll have a go.

To understand risk requires a flight of imagination. One has to imagine that an action is run as an experiment over and over again. This is sort of an unnatural mind game. It took humanity a long time to work out this mind game. The history of risk is brilliantly recounted in a book called *Against the Gods*,[26] which describes how different individuals created the theories, models and technologies for thinking about and measuring risk.

Risk was discovered by applying mathematics to the problems of gambling. Gambling is a 'perfect' mind game to model mathematically, because the rules of the game are set out in advance and are immutable for the duration of the game. So running a particular bet many times over, simulating it and counting the results reveals what its 'true' probability of winning is.

---

[26] *Against the Gods: The Remarkable Story of Risk* by Peter L. Bernstein, John Wiley and Sons, New York, 1996.

Some probabilities in some games are easy to work out. The probability of rolling a six-sided die and getting a 6 is 1 in 6. The probability of rolling two dice and getting a double six is 1/6 times 1/6 or 1 in 36. The probabilities in games like backgammon, poker or bridge are more complicated but can still be precisely quantified.

When the 'true' probability of an action can be quantified precisely, the action is said to be risky in a statistical sense. Rolling a die is risky because we cannot know what side it will land up on. But we know that if we play the 'mind game' or simulation and roll the die thousands of times that it has a 1 in 6 chance of rolling any particular number.

We can think of every action permitted by the rules of the game as taking place within a 'box'. The rules define the 'box'. Since we know the rules of a game, we can simulate what can happen inside the box. Even complex games like chess, which have enormous numbers of possible combinations of actions, can be simulated. The simulations are so complex they require powerful computers. But the simulations are now good enough to enable computer programs to beat chess Grand Masters.

Risk is the probability attaching to actions permitted under the rules. Uncertainty is what happens outside the box. Risk is measurable with the laws of probability if we know the rules. Uncertainty is, well, uncertain.

So how do I relate this definition of risk to your horse race example?

Well, in theory, we could run the mind game or simulate what might happen if we ran the horse in thousands of races. We could work out if the horse was best on hard or soft ground, short or long distances and so on. If this was a game, we would know all the rules and we could work out the probability of the horse winning in different conditions and make the odds accordingly.

In horse racing as in most real-life activities, we do not know all the rules of the game. There are more variables than we can measure and model. And there are uncertainties from 'outside the box' such as rider error, attempts at race fixing or attempts to drug the horses.

Is a horse race a good analogy for investment then?

In some respects it is a great analogy. In others, not.

Where it is neat is that it illustrates the subjectivity of prices. The odds that actually get offered on a particular horse are not just the result of a disinterested assessment of its chances of winning. They are also the result of the weight of money put down on the horse relative to the money put down on other horses. Bookmakers are making a market in the odds, and if a great deal of money goes onto one horse then the bookmakers will balance their books by adjusting the odds on the other horses.

A horse race is not a good analogy for investment because most investments are multi-period experiments. A horse race is a one-off experiment. So a bond will have a finite life and an equity an indefinite life. This is less like betting on one horse in one race than like betting on the racing performance of one horse over its entire career. With equities it is sort of like betting on the career performance of the horse and also of all of its progeny!

Betting on the racing performance of a horse over its entire career is not like modelling the probabilities of possible actions in a game. Over the life of the horse, the rules of the game may well change. Over the life of a business, the rules of the game are more likely to change than not. In some industries the 'horse' may be required to change into a 'cat' in order to survive!

So time is a source of uncertainty?

Time is a source of uncertainty but also of certainty. Insurance contracts are always written for a defined period of time. No one could afford to underwrite an indefinite number of rolls of the dice. You can model the likelihood of events in a defined period. Earthquake risk in California can be estimated for one year, but in geological time earthquakes are certain to take place. Over a very long time – like geological time – just about every conceivable event is likely to take place and is therefore 'certain'. So time is a paradox, a mystery!

Isn't market volatility a more conventional measure of risk?

Yes, statistical measures of market volatility are the conventional measure of risk, even the received wisdom. Market volatility is taken as a proxy for risk and has assumed great importance for several reasons. Financial theory, in particular the Capital Asset Pricing Model, says that returns correlate with market volatility. Indeed, the theory goes so far as to state that the key element of individual share price volatility which is rewarded with returns is the part that correlates with the overall volatility of the market. It states that, given certain assumptions, returns are proportional to the degree to which a share moves with the market. This statistical characteristic is the covariance of the share with the market divided by the variance of the market – also known as beta.

At another level, market volatility can be measured by the implied volatility in option prices. One measure of this is called the Vix – a measure of the implied volatility of S&P 500 options over the next month on an annualised basis. The Vix is an important measure of the perceptions of market risk. It is in a sense the price of risk.

What does market volatility measure?

At a statistical level market volatility is just a measure of the variances of prices from averages. It is more difficult to answer at a deeper level, at the level of the 'real' things that cause prices to vary. For example, many people can give you the statistical definition of beta. It is more difficult to say what it actually 'is'. Utilities stocks have lower betas and immature business models have higher betas. So beta seems to be affected by the volatility of cashflows and the requirement for net new capex – capex that must be funded by the market rather than out of the company's cashflows.

Why is the market risky or volatile?

I think the fundamental reason is related to time; it is a feature of duration mismatching. All investment is an effort to defeat the forces of time by creating and deploying capital. Capital involves maturity transformation: taking short-term real and financial assets and turning them into longer-term assets. This necessarily involves mismatching the duration of assets and liabilities. With no capital, no maturity mismatching and no markets we would all be living hand-to-mouth existences in hunter-gatherer type civilisations. As soon as financial and real capital is deployed, there is duration mismatching at many levels. There is an inter-generational mismatch – because human life is shorter than the life of some capital assets. Part of the duration mismatch is financial: the banking system has borrowed short and lent long or longer. Another mismatch arises from agency risk – the fact that individuals are not self-sufficient and do not hold personal balance sheets on which the duration of their assets and liabilities is matched. Individuals invest in 'collective investment schemes' like mutual funds, which invest in equities. The duration of the equities is indefinite but the individuals retain the freedom to sell and recover their capital on a few days' notice.

Is risk a 'soluble' problem then?

At a mundane, time-limited level we have worked out what many of the rules are. A basic rule is diversification. The rule was set out by Markowitz and states that if shares are not perfectly correlated, they can be combined in ways which create a portfolio with lower overall volatility than the individual shares. An 'efficient' portfolio is one where the return is maximised for a given level of risk. This insight is used to appraise different portfolios. The challenge is to increase returns without increasing volatility.

At a more fundamental level it is probably wise to accept that we do not actually know what the distribution of returns looks like, and that data for the last 200 years for the USA and UK may not be representative. We have market price data and returns derived from it – but this is meta data. The economic ecosystem only imperfectly measures the costs of and returns from natural and social assets. It may even be that these returns are not knowable in a precise monetary sense. There is always some irreducible risk, which is the unavoidable consequence of building up capital and therefore 'transforming maturities'. Significant discontinuities caused by natural and social 'revolutions' – for example, climate change, earthquake, war or political chaos – can transform the ability of assets to supply capabilities and hence make returns.

If we 'zoom out' to a macro or even a cosmic level, we test the frontiers of knowledge just as if we 'zoom in' to the micro or quantum mechanics level. Poetry may cope with uncertainty and interpret the mystery as well as anything.

The Persian mathematician Omar Khayyám described the system like this:

> 'For in and out, above, about, below,
> 'Tis nothing but a Magic Shadow-show,
> Play'd in a Box whose Candle is the Sun,
> Round which we Phantom figures come and go.'[27]

It seems as if we have to understand the 'rules' of a system before we can measure risk.

I think that's right. Mathematics has worked out the 'rules' for many systems. Gauss discovered the 'normal' or bell-shape distribution curve. Many things, like people's heights, are 'normally' distributed, meaning that there are as many very tall people as very short people and that the 'distribution' of heights on either side of the average height is symmetrical. If you know or have reason to believe that a variable is normally distributed, you can use statistical rules to infer the characteristics of an entire population from a sample. For the heights of people, statistical rules will tell you the 'risk' or likelihood that a given person will be within a certain distance, measured in 'standard deviations', of the average. These statistical rules work very well with physical variables because the rules or models which govern the behaviour of physical variables are often independent of time and are immutable – allowing very accurate predictions.

Military war planners play war games to model different strategies for war. They put into the model everything they know about their own side's capabilities and all their intelligence about the other side's capabilities. But the model cannot cover every conceivable contingency. There will always remain residual 'unk unks', also known as the 'unknown unknowns'.

---

[27] *The Rubáiyát of Omar Khayyám*, translated by Edward Fitzgerald.

Are the 'rules' of financial systems understood?

Hmmm! Modern civilisation is probably more conceited than its forbears where financial systems are concerned! This is partly because economics has itself become a religion and its assumptions are therefore less often questioned. Modern civilisation thinks it understands the financial system. This may be a bit of a conceit.

Why's that?

What is new about the modern financial system *vis à vis* its predecessors is the quantity of data and the ease with which it is available. Before computing power was cheap, financial data was scarce and very expensive. What is the nature of this financial data? It is mainly *price* data. Stock exchanges store massive quantities of price data for underlying stocks and bonds and for derivatives of those securities, like indices. So a researcher asking a question like, 'What is the return on equities?' can apply statistical science to a mass of price data and arrive at an apparently precise and convincing answer.

What's wrong with that?

At one level there's nothing wrong with it – provided one understands its limitations. Price data is not 'fundamental' data in the same way that a controlled experiment in physics or chemistry is 'fundamental'. Prices capture all sorts of influences, which are extremely difficult to disentangle. One of the problems with price is that the economic system that creates prices is not a 'sealed system'. There are all sorts of 'leaks'. One leak is the ability to borrow from the future by creating more credit. Another leak is the discovery and exploitation of 'new' natural resources, which accounting treats as a 'free' input. As a result, prices are like 'history' – not always very scientific in the sense of not providing a reliable basis for predictions. Despite this, people in financial markets regularly take price histories, perform complicated statistical manipulations on them and deduce that a certain event should occur on average, say, 'once every 100 years'.

Can't we look at fundamental data rather than price data?

People look at the data that is available rather than seek to create new data. Creating data is expensive and after the event may be impossible. The main frameworks for capturing financial data are corporate accounting models and national accounting models. So people take accounting data and use it as if it were fundamental data.

What's wrong with corporate accounting data?

Again, there's nothing wrong with it provided one accepts it for what it is. Corporate accounts only record things as 'assets' if they are considered likely to convert into cash. Once it is considered that they will not convert to cash, the asset is taken out of the 'population' of assets. Assets come into and out of the corporate accounting system depending on current opinion of their ability to generate cash. Quite of lot assets that someone takes the credit for 'creating' are really assets created by someone else that are just being 'recycled'.

So can we measure the risk of financial assets?

Yes, we can. But not with the same level of certainty as with physical variables. It is easier to be 'fooled by randomness'.

What do you mean by that?

Financial experiments are more difficult to perform than physical experiments. It is more difficult to know if one has correctly understood the rules of the system. Suppose that you bought a bond and your model told you that there was a 5% risk of the bond defaulting. The bond therefore pays a premium over some 'risk-free' rate of interest. Suppose the bond redeems on its due date. Does this prove that your model was correct? It is easy to believe that it does. But to prove the model requires the ability to run the simulation many times. And you have only run it in real life once. If the issuer goes bust six months after you got redeemed, it is quite possible that the model was miles wrong and that you were just lucky. And it is much more difficult to model the risk of an equity share than a bond.

So is it possible to model the risk of an equity share?

There are basically two approaches: the Ben Graham approach and the statistical approach, of which the Capital Asset Pricing Model is one variant.

The Ben Graham approach is essentially cautious and uses a comparison of price versus value to assess risk. This statement from *The Intelligent Investor*[28] encapsulates much of his approach:

> '*Additionally, we hope to implant in the reader a tendency to measure or quantify. For 99 issues out of 100 we could say that at some price they are cheap enough to buy and at some other price they would be so dear that they should be sold.*'

The Ben Graham approach to value is conservative – based entirely on cash and using accounts as the main window onto what the cash surpluses are likely to be.

In the Graham approach, price is like a bid made in a round of bridge. Where the cards are located around the table – that is, which player holds which cards – is where objectively the 'value' lies. There are some bids that involve no risk because if the bid is the highest bid, the tricks will be won easily. And there are other bids that are certain to lose. In the Graham approach, economic value is the (present) value of the sum of the cash surpluses that will come out of a business. Graham only looks at the components

---

[28] *The Intelligent Investor* by Benjamin Graham, first published in 1949.

of economic value that are relatively objective within a tolerance – like balance sheet net cash and net worth, historic earnings. Graham's approach is very tolerant of 'not knowing'. If you don't know, you don't play the game. To a large extent the destiny or success or failure of an investment is predetermined by the relationship of the price paid to the economic value.

The statistical approach is 'normative' – it is premised on what is supposed to be 'normal'. Governments normally do not go bust and their bonds are normally relatively 'risk-free', equities are risky and should normally earn a risk premium and so on. The approach is impressive because it is supported by data – in quantities which are so vast only computers can handle it – and by theories which are 'beautiful' in the sense of being logically coherent.

Which is better?

Both have their advantages and disadvantages. People who have followed the Ben Graham approach, like Warren Buffett, have ended up making superior returns. People who have followed the statistical approach have raised a lot of assets, not least because people like logic and lots of data!

So why do price and value diverge?

Uncertainty. If everyone knew the rules then the risk could be calculated and price and value would not get very far apart. Since the rules, the shapes of the statistical distribution of the data, are not altogether known there's plenty of room for price and value to differ.

Isn't value more certain than price?

The variability of prices around their means – their standard deviations are probably wider than the variability of values around their means. But I suppose one has to say that price and value are equally uncertain since they are reflexive to a large extent.

Can't we estimate how risky economic value is?

Yes, there are lots of factors that we can look at which, all else being equal, tend to increase or decrease the risk inherent in any given value. But the degree of precision is not the same as for physical variables.

We can put value on a spectrum from almost risk-free to extremely risky. A first cut categorisation is by 'asset class'. The lowest risk asset is cash. Then, as we go out in time, risk increases. So short-dated bonds are not so risky. Long-dated bonds are risky. And equities as irredeemables are very risky. But although equities prices tend to move together, equities are very heterogeneous, which makes generalisation more difficult.

So time is a key determinant of risk?

Yes. As we go out into the future, risk increases for all assets because the potential for value to diverge from price grows. Even cash becomes risky over longer periods, because it can devalue against real assets and against other currencies. In other words, cash is only risk-free in the long run in nominal terms. At least with cash it usually takes a long time to lose most of your money.

It is also the case that the potential for return increases as we go out in time. This is the attraction of finding 'growth' stocks – business models which can grow by replicating a 'formula'.

How do we discriminate between financial assets which have apparently similar durations?

Categorizing assets by their durations helps to make it possible to compare apples with apples. But duration alone is not enough. Not all ten-year bonds are equally risky, and although equities are all in principle irredeemable, their risk varies greatly.

A second cut is to separate out 'financial assets' from 'real assets'. Financial assets like bonds have durations that can be known with a high degree of certainty. The duration of real assets is harder to appraise.

A third cut is to categorise equities by archetypal business model. Some archetypal business models are generically riskier than others. Lending and capital goods business models are at the risky end of the spectrum. Service and distribution business models are at the less risky end of the spectrum.

A fourth cut categorisation is to group equities by the age or 'maturity' of their business projects. Most immature businesses are riskier than mature businesses.

A fifth cut is to look at capital structure. Projects carrying a lot of debt are risky.

A sixth cut is to look at the cash surpluses and how certain they are. At the almost risk-free end, there's net worth that is represented by cash that is on the balance sheet or which can be realised by selling existing, on-balance-sheet, saleable assets. At the extremely risky end of the spectrum are cashflows from business projects which have negligible realisable net assets and no near-term cash surpluses where the value is all contingent on the success of an immature business model.

You made fun of financial intermediaries asking their clients for their 'attitude to risk'.

The difficulty with the 'attitude to risk' question is that the client may have to take a psychometric test to come up with an objective answer. And even if he knew the answer, paradoxically the most valuable use to which the client could put the information might be to do the opposite of his natural preference. So a risk-averse client might be well advised to take a bit more risk and vice versa.

Are there questions you can ask which a client can answer objectively?

Well, I suppose all the answers are to some extent subjective. A very wealthy person may be insecure and think of himself as poor and vice versa. That said, there are some questions which can be more objectively answered like: How long do you want to hold this investment? What is the most you can afford to lose in absolute terms? What sort of maximum 'draw' or downside can you tolerate in any 12-month period?

You said that my attitude to the future mattered more than my attitude to risk. Is that really true?

It is sort of a tautological statement! Without a future, there's not much risk. And the risks that exist or that you perceive to exist are greatly influenced by your theory of the future.

Risk

'Your task is not to foresee the future but to make it possible.'

– Hervé Bazin

'The immediately possible is hardly worth living for. It is the ideal that kindles enthusiasm and gives inspiration and vigour to all human effort.'

– Quoted by Lord Denning to his eldest brother who was killed in WW1

'... it is not present expectations that correspond to future events but future events which are shaped by present expectations.'

– George Soros in *The Alchemy of Finance*

'The social object of skilled investment should be to defeat the dark forces of time and ignorance which envelop our future.'

– J.M. Keynes in *The General Theory*

CHAPTER 10

The future

What do you mean by 'a theory about the future'?

Everyone has a theory about the future. You may not think
about it, but you do have a theory about the future. The skill is
to exteriorise and test the theory.

Why do you say that?

Maybe assumption is a better word than theory. Everything
we do is based on assumptions. For example, we may not
know how to change a car tyre. But we have a conscious or
subconscious theory about punctures. Our theory might be
that we don't think it will happen to us, that we think we will
be able to call for assistance, that we reckon we will work
out how to change the tyre if the problem arises and so on.
Our theory might even be that it is not an important enough
problem to have a theory about. What are your assumptions
about the future?

**To be honest, I don't explicitly think about it all that often.
You could say that the future is something that happens while
I am thinking about something else!**

Then maybe you are assuming that the future will be like the
past. Maybe that's not an unreasonable assumption?

Except that when I think of the life my grandparents and great-grandparents lived it was very, very different from my own.

How so?

The mass transport of my great-grandfather's childhood was the ocean-going liner and the railway, not cars and aeroplanes. Cars were a niche product. My great-grandmother's first 'driving lesson' was to drive a pony and trap. My father's grandfather never learnt to drive a car. The long-distance communications technology of that time was the telegraph not the telephone. The penetration of electrification was still quite low. Television and nuclear power had not been invented. The computer had not been invented. The chemicals industry had not yet invented most of the plastics we use.

Yes, the past is a different country and it is difficult to get back into the minds of these bygone worlds.

How do you think that the world will change during the rest of my life?

There is a saying that the future already exists, but is just unevenly distributed. This means that we don't not need to speculate about things that do not currently exist, so much as speculate about what currently exists and will become adopted by more people and businesses.

Existing trends that are likely to continue include:

- the further roll-out of electrification around the world – a process that has been progressing over the last 100 years,

- continued roll-out of information technology,

- increasing concern for the environment; governments are likely to try to impose economic costs on environmental damage,

- increasing energy costs to incentivise investment in alternative 'green' energy sources such as wind and solar, and

- rising transport costs as energy, metal and pollution costs rise.

There is more research, data collection, and information creation going on today than at any point in human history, which suggests that the rate of change in the infrastructure of civilisation will continue to be high.

Are there any 'mega trends' which will persist for years?

We and our parents have lived with and through a number of mega trends. Some are likely to persist and some will quite likely reach a turning point in the next few decades.

One centuries-old trend is the 'roll out' of what is loosely called 'capitalism' and which is a hotchpotch of property rights, financial systems, markets, regulation and technology. Although capitalism is not one system, the common element in all capitalistic systems is 'the market'. As Churchill said of democracy, capitalism is a lousy system but no one has come up with a better one.

Another old trend is population growth. This has been remarkable. World population has grown from around two billion around 1900 to nearly seven billion now. Projections suggest a population of around nine billion by 2050 is possible. Population growth presents many problems.

A trend that may be peaking is per capita consumption of hydrocarbons in developed economies. Much of global economic growth in the last 50 years may be less attributable to brilliant economic policy than to the abundance of cheap hydrocarbons. Cheap and growing supply of hydrocarbons and roll-out of computer technology probably explain most of the 'productivity' improvements in the last 50 years.

Another trend that may have peaked in developed economies and may still have a long way to go in emerging markets is the growth of per capita credit. The total amount of credit in many developed economies has shown dramatic growth in the last 25 years up to 2008. Deregulation of financial markets and benign commodity prices caused much of the growth. Developed economies will now adjust to much slower rates of credit growth – in some cases, credit contraction.

Is it possible to *value* the future?

Yes. That is what civilisation implicitly does. Consciously and subconsciously civilisation is valuing the future.

It does this in many ways. Most obviously it does it by creating property (or appropriating it from or to Nature and society) and it creates prices for property. Prices all express some view of the future.

Some of the property is very explicitly defined and priced. Debt and equity capital is rather precisely defined and when it is traded prices are created.

Every day, markets for financial capital, for debt and equity, are producing estimates of the expected future cashflows from specific bonds and equities and are putting values on them. The total value of debt outstanding is expected to be repaid – if not at par value then at least at the current market value. These bond values explicitly value the future – the future cashflows the bond is expected to produce. The sum total of the capitalisations of all of the companies quoted on the Stock Exchange, their share prices multiplied by the number of shares in issue, is an estimate of the total amount of cash which those businesses will return to their shareholders by way of profits and return *of* invested capital.

Since the investment process is continuous and the composition of the universe of quoted bonds and companies changes over time it is difficult to compare the expected cash surpluses, the market capitalisations, with the subsequent outcomes. This sort of historical 'cash on cash' or historical cash return on market capitalisation is a different way of appraising market efficiency; but it is difficult to do and seldom attempted.

Surely this is only valuing part of reality?

Yes. Law and property, assets and accounting capture a big chunk of civilisation but only a subset of reality.

Many common or garden 'assets' are outside the legal system and outside the accounting system. Is a wild animal someone's property? Legal systems tend to regard them as someone's property if they are *on* someone's property. But some of them, like whales or geese, travel around the world. They aren't on anyone's balance sheet. Their future is not valued by the economic ecosystem at all. The loss of 'value' caused by the extinction of a species is not measured. The loss of an entire ecosystem or micro-climate barely moves the political and economic needle in large countries and is treated as if irrelevant when it happens in other countries.

And then there's non-physical or metaphysical reality, states of being, what to choose to believe in or not. These things are valuable but difficult to value directly in the 'for-money' economy.

But aren't all the different futures inter-linked?

Within the economic ecosystem the prices of all assets are correlated. The prices of all financial assets are correlated because they all depend on the availability of money and credit. Banks within a monetary system are all interlinked. The individual balance sheets are 'roped together' like climbers on a mountain. If one falls, everyone is affected. In the 2008 banking crisis the prices of almost all asset classes dropped in the short term, even gold. The prices of all 'real' assets are inter-linked because it is the monetary and credit system which provides the pricing system.

Capitalist financial systems are sometimes characterised as individualistic and selfish as opposed to collectivist and communal. But capitalist systems also mutualise profits and losses in a variety of ways. One way is through the tax and social security systems. Another way is through inflation which spreads the cost of impaired credit across an entire economy.

A Holy Grail in investment is to find 'non-correlated' assets which can reduce the risk of portfolios. International diversification has historically reduced risk. But the increasing integration of the global economy has increased mutual interdependence across national boundaries.

The financial links between the futures of different assets and countries are pretty obvious because they are measurable in money terms. The ecological links, the changes in, say, the climate in one part of the world caused by activity in another part of the world, are not measured in terms of money and have been variously denied, belittled or ignored.

It seems as if some form of 'world government' is required!

Some form of 'world law' is needed and to some extent it already exists. Many countries subscribe to the General Agreement on Tariffs and Trade and the World Trade Organisation.

Some problems can only be solved by collaboration. As the saying goes, if we are all in the same boat, it does not matter much if the hole is at your end or mine. We have a mutual interest in pumping. If people were able to choose between world government and world war most people, one would hope, would choose world government.

In some respects the idea of world government runs against a centuries old Anglo-Saxon tradition of *laissez faire*. The philosophy of Adam Smith has provided justification and comfort for the notion that if 'everyone minds their own business' then the collective result will be just fine.

Surely someone is responsible for the future?

Everyone and no one.

Everyone contributes to the future whether consciously or subconsciously, through their knowledge or their ignorance. Reality is full of fine intentions and unintended consequences, bold visions and mistaken beliefs, brave hopes and misplaced trust.

For most practical purposes building the future is left to three sorts of organisations: businesses operating in the exchange economy; governments which straddle the exchange and the 'not-for-money' economies; and the Churches which straddle the metaphysical and physical worlds.

The exchange economy produces prices for financial and real assets which implicitly value large parts of the future. Government seeks to regulate and direct the exchange economy in order to produce more 'meaningful' prices. 'Better prices', which usually means prices justified by competitive supply and demand, create a 'better' allocation of resources.

Government also reserves the right to 'play by its own rules' when it suits it, for example, in time of war. The rules for government accounting are different from the rules for corporations. By commercial standards government accounts are not very meaningful. Most government accounting is cash accounting which has no concept of capital. As a result much government is profligate with capital and turns a blind eye to the inter-temporal wealth transfers which are taking place all the time. Pools of natural, social and economic capital created in the past are consumed in the present without any form of accountability. It suits government not to have proper accounts. Expenses can be run up against arcane account headings like 'the committee for the re-election of the president'. Often even the insiders have no idea what is in these accounts.

Although government is supposed to operate within the law the legislature has the power to change the law if the law does not suit the government.

Do businesspeople, politicians and Churchmen understand the system?

While they all understand their own specialisms, how many of them have an informed view of the direction in which civilisation is headed? Economics and business have become Gods in the Pantheon of Western civilization. Yet theologians of the main 'faith groups', Christianity, Islam or Judaism, study the sacred texts of their own religions and are seldom competent to discuss the 'sacred' texts of modern financial economics, government and corporate financial statements. Economists seldom consider the role of religion in economic policy, even though Max Weber pointed out the importance of the Protestant or Puritan 'work ethic' in Western economic culture and development. Professional politicians are often better versed in vote catching issues such as immigration than they are in the workings of the economic ecosystem. As Richard Feynman said, 'In this age of specialization men who thoroughly know one field are often incompetent to discuss another'.

Do many businesspeople, politicians or clerics understand the wider economy and the hierarchy of basic business models required to make the economy work? The financial system is directly responsible for creating money and credit and therefore obviously responsible for creating explicit futures. When the credit which banks and their customers have created turns out to have been based on false premises, its value collapses. When 'credit bubbles' burst the reaction of the anti-establishment parties is schadenfreude while the Establishment behaves with the indignation of Trustafarians when they discover that their living allowance has been cut. How many people know how much the money supply expanded from one election to the next and what the additional credit was allocated to? How many politicians agitate for 'whole of government' accounts without which it is difficult to hold government to account?

It falls to politicians at all levels, which means everyone in a democracy, to try to reconcile the demands of the present with hopes and visions for the future. Politics is supposed to be about visions of the future and policies to get there from the present. Politics ought to be a disinterested examination of the merits of policies but can deteriorate into a 'blame game'. The future envisioned may be nothing nobler than achieving re-election in five years' time.

Churches are supposed to concern themselves with the spiritual more than the temporal, the individual more than the organisation, conscience more than consumption. They are now increasingly superseded by the advertising industry, which manipulates the collective psyche on behalf of its clients.

Is 'capitalism' to blame for the shortcomings of the 'pricing system'?

Ironically some concept of capital is essential for any pricing system to work. Without some notion of capital it is impossible to estimate 'fair' inter-temporal prices.

How's that?

Suppose we take an asset like a nation's oil reserves. How should a country 'value' its oil reserves? It can sidestep the question and just produce as much oil as possible. Or it can consciously decide that oil reserves are a finite resource and that the current generations should not consume all the proceeds of oil production in the present.

The Oil Ministry of Norway sends representatives to investor conferences who explain that Norwegian government policy recognises that their oil is a wasting asset. The Norwegian government explicitly seeks to set aside a proportion of its oil revenues and invests it in a sovereign wealth fund to provide for future generations. The natural asset is recognised for what it is: natural capital. The financial asset, the sovereign wealth fund, is used to preserve capital so that future generations may also benefit.

Norway's policy might be characterised as 'socialist capitalism'. A key reason why it works is that Norway is a price taker in the oil market and the capital markets. It is not in a position to rig the market.

What do you mean?

Well, your question was about the 'shortcomings of the pricing system'.

To create some form of 'pricing system' property, like oil production rights, needs to be fairly well spread or 'fragmented' and the owners need to be able to trade freely with each other to establish prices. At the very least, ownership and regulation need to be separated.

Communist systems also have a concept of capital. They tend to believe that capital should all be owned by the State. Some of the State officials may have high ideals about how the capital should be deployed. The inherent conflicts of interest where the State is the owner, manager, distributor and buyer of, say, oil meant the reality fell far short of the aspiration. Monopolies are not capable of self-regulation.

At a practical level what should I invest in?

The most succinct answer to that question at all levels is that one should invest in the things where the gap between value and price is greatest. In the 'not-for-money' economy this may mean your children, spouse, wider family and friends. The most valuable investment in the 'not-for-money economy' is time rather than money.

Price–value gaps exist everywhere. Jeremy Gilley set up an organisation called Peace One Day to promote an annual Day of Peace each 21 September. This charity seeks to address a gap so enormous that it has eluded civilisation for centuries if not millennia. Ironically the price–value gap is also large in politics, which is a minority sport distained by the majority.

Price–value gaps in financial securities are generally of smaller orders of magnitude but can still be very large. Some investors made billions by going short of securitised mortgages in the USA when they believed that these assets were greatly over-valued. Other investors have made fortunes backing specific business products and trends, like Bill Gates with the PC operating system or Larry Ellison with the relational database.

Aren't some price–value gaps riskier than others?
That must be true.

It is hard to know if some prices are the 'right' prices. That's because the consequences of some activities are difficult to estimate or anticipate. One can make an argument that the consequences of fossil fuel consumption include climate change and pollution and that these things are not in the price. If coal and oil are systematically underpriced then current generations pay too little and future generations may suffer climate change and economic collapse.

The difficulty with individual risks is to know where they rank in the overall 'cascade' of risks and the degree of inter-relationship or correlation between the different risks. The price of a currency, its exchange rates with other currencies, ranks rather high. Other high ranking risks like the solvency of a government may only be imperfectly priced by the bond markets. Although there may be a price in the market it may not mean very much. Prices lose their meaning when it is very difficult to trade meaningful volumes at the price quoted, when liquidity evaporates very fast. The securities of individual companies rank rather low in the cascade of risks.

In the serendipitous economy described by Adam Smith individual economic units each pursuing their own interests create a socially acceptable overall result. The 'real world' is a good deal less than perfect. Some values elude pricing. Some prices only barely approximate to value. Gaps between price and value can be sustained for years.

Some risks elude reliable estimation even after the event. In other words, it may never be possible to know in a statistical sense if the risk was worth taking. Wars often fall into this category. The losing side in a war usually seems to have taken a bad decision. But it is also difficult to know if the winning side necessarily took an acceptable risk. Was Britain right to honour its treaty obligations and enter WW1 against Germany after Germany invaded Belgium? Was the USA right to invade Iraq and depose Sadaam Hussein? Since the possible alternative histories are unknown, analysis of these risks is not objective.

Is it necessary to take a view on these sorts of general trends?

A chartist might tell you that you need to look at the price history. A fundamental analyst might tell you that what counts is the 'intrinsic value'. A macro fund manager might tell you that the macroeconomic variables, like the credit cycle, government policy and exchange rates, were most important.

In practice an investment in any financial asset implicitly expresses a mix of micro and macro views. If you buy a short-dated bond issued by a specific country, you implicitly take an investment view on a small number of things – mainly currency risk, but also interest rate and credit risk.

If you buy the equity of a multinational business, you are implicitly taking an investment view on a complicated cocktail of different variables and trends. A few of the variables will usually dominate the overall result. When you buy an equity in a retailer in an emerging market, it often turns out that the overall result is dominated by the movement in the currency of the country in which the business operates. When you buy an equity in an industry making a commodity which is relatively undifferentiated, say copper, it often turns out that the overall result is dominated by the change in the copper price – which in turn affects the structure and evolution of production capacity relative to demand.

One does not have to be right about all the general trends. One just needs to make sure that the implicit odds in the price paid for a specific investment are sufficiently long versus your own sense of the odds; that is, that risks on the future are sufficiently reflected to leave a margin of error, or, as Ben Graham put it, a 'margin of safety'.

Afterword

To introduce the subject of investment, I wrote an imaginary dialogue between a financial adviser, more of an old-fashioned bank manager-type than a typical financial adviser, and a young man at the start of his career. The upshot was *Valuing the Future*, which I have turned into a book.

Implicit in the dialogue is the underlying question, '*Why* should I invest?' It may well be true that most people think finance and investment is boring. They are more interested in investing their time in non-financial activities: decorating the house, following their football club, bringing up children, travelling.

Most people will understand anything if they are sufficiently interested. The critical ingredient is motivation. Any subject can be boring if there is no motive for studying it. Should anyone invest? Why? What are the motivations for investment?

It is taken as axiomatic in social psychology and in economics that people are self-interested. Economists find it self-evident that people act in their own interests. It may be true that everyone is self-interested. It is less obvious that everyone knows what is in their own best interests, that everyone has the knowledge to make an informed choice or has access to the necessary information.

Although it may be in people's self-interest to understand financial investment, most people do not hold financial investments. According to a report from the Office for National Statistics in the UK, for example:

> 'Half of all households in Britain had gross financial wealth of £7,200 or less and net financial wealth of £5,200 or less. The analysis also shows that 25 per cent of households had net financial wealth that was negligible: a large number of households at the lower end of the distribution had negligible, zero or negative net financial wealth.'[29]

Half of all UK households had wealth in pension schemes of less than £29,200 in 2006/08.

There's an apparent paradox. Although it is in people's self-interest to invest, half of all households in the UK do not have significant financial assets. Why is this? In a relatively wealthy country like the UK, poverty is not the main reason. Nor is it that people do not wish to invest, or that the UK is unrepresentative. A similar phenomenon exists in most countries.

Most people want to build something for the future and everyone is investing their time in something – financial or non-financial – all the time. My surmise is that most people do not buy financial assets for two main reasons: lack of trust, and lack of time to get comfortable with what they are buying. The difficulty people confront when they want to make a financial investment is that the 'system' is so big and impersonal that they do not have confidence either in it, or in their understanding of it.

Trust is essential in investment because the financial investments that individuals make are *indirect* rather than direct. Financial investment is at several removes from the purchase and operation of real, non-financial assets. The chain of interfaces

---

[29] Office for National Statistics, 'Wealth in Great Britain, 2006/08'.

is long and a high level of trust and integrity is essential for the system to work. For example, an individual puts his money into a bank account and the bank uses it to buy a range of financial assets. Behind the financial assets are the financial liabilities of the bank's counterparties and behind those financial liabilities – sometimes a long way behind – are real assets in the form of buildings, trained people and know-how.

Faced with uncertainty, many people often start out by turning to a so-called Independent Financial Adviser or IFA. IFAs are intermediaries who sell financial products that are supplied by finance businesses, the 'manufacturers' or the creators of the financial product. In the 'old days' financial advisers were wholly remunerated on a commission basis. This structural conflict of interest meant that the IFA was consciously or subconsciously biased towards the conclusion that the customer should indeed invest in the product that yielded the IFA the highest commission! Commission was often directly related to the value of the premiums paid over. If the IFA 'made the sale', 30 per cent, 40 per cent or even 100 per cent of the first year's premium on an endowment savings product was typically paid over to the adviser by the manufacturer. In the 'old, old days', which were not long ago, the adviser did not even have to disclose to the buyer how much commission he was going to receive as a result of the sale. Very often, the commission bore no relationship to the quality of the advice given. In financial services the customers were sold product, rather than buying with discrimination.

Many people bought endowment saving products in the UK and felt they were getting a good deal because the IFA 'generously' rebated half the commission to the customer in cash. This sales gimmick was, of course, only a 'come-on'. In exchange, the customer agreed to a number of onerous commitments against which the come-on looks ridiculously small: to pay a monthly sum across to the savings company for the next 25 years; to lose a significant proportion of the capital handed over in the event of early cancellation; to accept all the investment risk without having any influence over the investment policy. The customer made a commitment stretching out over most of a working lifetime. The IFA walked away with cash in hand and almost no future obligations.

The British public has a much higher proportion of its wealth invested in property than in financial assets. Given the inherent distrust of financial services, and the significant tax advantages of investment in home ownership (zero capital gains tax), it is not difficult to understand this preference for real estate. As it happens, over the ten years to 2009, returns on residential property in the UK were higher than on any other asset class. So the preference for property has been rewarded in recent history. Whether returns on residential property will be as good in the next ten years, given reversion to the mean and the change in the availability of loans secured on property, is another matter.

The views of the money adviser in the dialogue in *Valuing the Future* differ from those of a typical IFA. He has some advantages. He does not have any products to sell. He does not need to fill out a questionnaire about his customer's attitude to risk in order to satisfy his compliance department or his professional indemnity insurance policy. He does not have to look at tax and tax incentives. He is just offering his opinion about investment in general.

This freedom from having to sell a product allows the adviser to delve into some of the broader questions. As a result, the conversation ranges over a broad area beyond the specifics of a particular contract. The adviser makes a number of generalisations, which are necessarily simplifications. As it is a conversation, the underlying complications are not all explored in detail. Rather than peddling simple nostrums, the conversation is intended to encourage curiosity about some of the complications that underlie investment.

Glossary

Common or garden assets	Assets in common parlance are often owned by no one in particular and generate no cash. Common assets are things appreciated just by standing and staring – like Nature. Natural assets include things like mountains and oceans, rivers, animals and plants. Natural assets are celebrated by poets – like the author of the Psalms of David. Society or civilisation also creates 'social' assets which are owned in common like languages or legal systems.
	Assets may be physical or metaphysical like truth, goodness and beauty.
Time	A fundamental feature of existence. One feature of time is that nothing physical persists unchanged forever, although relatively, some things persist for very long periods. From the perspective of one person the past and the future only exist in the present and within the context of a civilisation. Time may be a divine experiment and is certainly a mystery.
Civilisation	A man-made system to organise resources and to create capabilities for delivering a flow of resources across time.
Capital	A stock which persists through several periods of time rather than a flow which expires or is consumed in one period. Real capital is stuff, physical or intangible, which exists. If someone can claim

ownership of the real capital it can be used as the implicit collateral or explicit security for financial capital. Financial capital is a representation of real capital created by civilisation for the purpose of organising and managing real capital.

Property

An ownership claim on a resource.

Private ownership and market exchange are the systems on which Western civilisation is built. Adam Smith argued that the rational, calculated choices of individuals regarding their own property created acceptable social order.

Orthodox 'Victorian' economics considered that the private calculation of costs and benefits of voluntary exchange were consistent with public costs and benefits.

Victorian orthodoxy was challenged by mass unemployment in the first half of the 20th century and awareness of large scale ecological destruction in the second half of the century.

Utopian alternatives under various guises promising better management under public ownership, for example Communism, have produced lower living standards and political oppression.

Money

A system for transferring property created by banks and their customers.

Money is a derivative of 'real' assets created by the banking system. It has fundamentally paradoxical aspects: if everyone held their money in cash, the banking system would collapse; if all the banks and their customers prefer to hold money rather than lend and invest then economic activity collapses.

This surreal situation was described by Keynes in *The General Theory* in terms of green cheese:

'Unemployment develops... because people want the Moon; – men cannot be employed when the object of desire (i.e. money) is something which cannot be produced and demand for which cannot be readily choked off. There is no remedy but to persuade the public that green cheese is practically the same thing and to have a green cheese factory (i.e. a central bank) under public control.'

| Value | Temporal and material value derives from access to resources. Metaphysical value might be summarised as 'truth, goodness and beauty'. |

| Economics | Man-made models for understanding how human activity is organised to deliver resources. Microeconomics models how prices are formed; macroeconomics models how categories of economic unit interact, for example government, finance businesses, non-finance businesses, consumers and so on. |

Alfred Marshall at Cambridge laid much of the foundations of microeconomics. Wicksell and Keynes laid the foundations of macroeconomics.

In 1949 Keynes gave this toast at a dinner of the Royal Economic Society: 'I give you the toast of the Royal Economic Society, of economics and economists, who are the trustees, not of civilisation, but of the possibility of civilisation.'

| Economic 'ecosystem' | The man-made political, social, legal, engineering and economic systems which create real and financial capital and deliver a 'standard of living'. The economic ecosystem is both managed and self-organising. The economic ecosystem depends on the natural ecosystem which it takes for granted but is not always in harmony with. |

| Economic value | Economic value is a system for measuring the productivity of financial capital. |

| Economic value of a company | A combination of pvs of existing projects and npvs of follow-on or new projects which have yet to start. A synonym for pv. |

What you notionally get from a business aka 'intrinsic value', 'conceptual pv'	Conceptual pv is necessarily subjective. Some of the most important subjective elements are whether management can deliver the projects to time and to budget, the size of the potential market opportunities, the competitive advantage of the business, and capital intensity of the projects
Economic asset or liability	Economic assets are a subset of natural and social assets which produce returns measured in terms of money.
Present value (pv) aka 'economic value'	Present value usually means present value of future cashflows to shareholders (equity). Present value is sometimes used to mean the pv of the future cashflows to a project rather than to equity – in other words of the cashflows of the project available for the providers of debt and equity capital.

Pv is a gross number comprising the return of the capital invested and the additional npv achieved over and above invested capital.

PV future cashflows = invested capital + npv of projects.

A project pv, that is the pv of the cashflows to a project, can be split into the pv attributable to the providers of debt and equity. The equity pv is the residual after prior claims have been deducted from project pv.

Pv may be shown pre- or post-tax. Investors are interested in the post-tax figures.

Pv can only be known with certainty after the event.

Npv is a net number, comprised of the pv (the gross cashflows to the project or to the equity) less the invested capital. Npv, cumulative profits and cumulative cashflow are all identical after the event.

Net present value (npv)	Present value of future cashflows less past cash invested in the capital cost of the project.

Npv is also equal to the present value of future net profits which are equal to the future net cashflows. Npv like pv can only be known with certainty after the event.

Accounting asset or liability	Something which exists at a given time and is owned by a specific legal or natural person and which is expected to give rise to a flow of money or money's worth in the future.
	Assets are written into and out of accounts according to accounting conventions regarding their recoverability in cash.
	Accounting conventions have been created to provide simple and practical ways of coping with uncertainty. For example, it cannot be known with complete certainty whether a capital good will generate a return in the future. So by convention the asset is recorded at cost and the validity of this assumption is reconsidered at each subsequent balance sheet date.
	Liabilities are just negative assets.
Financial asset or liability	An asset defined in terms of the amount of money or cash it will deliver in the future.
	Common categories of financial assets include bonds, trade debtors and creditors, also known as receivables, and payables.
	More complicated categories include pension rights and leases.
Equity	An ownership claim.
Also known as: owner's equity, shareholders' equity, equity capital, capital or ownership interest	An equity is a liability by convention only.
	Equity may refer to any ownership interest but in investment it usually refers to ownership of shares in limited liability companies.
	Share ownership is a peculiar and paradoxical form of ownership in which:

- collections of business assets are owned and managed in limited liability corporations separately from the personal assets of the ultimate owners,
- the costs and benefits of ownership of the projects in the corporate entity are mutualised among the shareholders – but not with the rest of society,

- the liability of the owners for any losses of the business is limited to the amount of capital originally subscribed, and

- in exchange for a share, which gives part ownership of the company, the company gives a promise to divide and distribute profits at some indeterminate time in the future subject to the existence of sufficient cash and legally defined distributable profits and to the discretion/whim of the directors.

Equity in particular projects may turn out to have large or little pv.

The collective value of quoted equities provides a shop window in which a view of the economic value of the future is reflected.

Real asset   An asset other than a financial asset. Real assets may be economic; that is, they give rise to money values such as a building which is let out or uneconomic. They have no cash value, such as the Sun, the Moon and the stars.

Opportunity cost A system for valuing real and financial assets by reference to their alternative uses.

Maturity   The repayment date for a financial asset.

Duration   The average time to payment of a stream of cashflows. So, a conventional bond which matures after five years might make five annual payments to its owner: interest in each of the first four years and interest and capital in year five. Duration is the weighted average time to payment. Duration is calculated using the 'present' or discounted future values of the cash payments rather than the future or 'actual' cash payments.

Yield curve   A line which plots spot interest rates against maturities of bonds in the same class (for example, government bonds with equivalent credit ratings)

Credit   A legal contract in which some material part of the
                  performance of the contract takes place at some point in
                  the future rather than immediately – thereby requiring
                  an element of trust in execution of the contract.

Business project A collection of real assets and repeatable processes
                  operated by management and financed with a capital
                  structure including equity to deliver a market need
                  whilst delivering economic value for shareholders. A
                  business project may be owned by a limited liability
                  company, owned in partnership or by a sole trader.

Business model   The architecture of the system of systems which
                  organises the various processes inside a business
                  to take inputs and deliver product whilst creating
                  economic value. Products and business models can be
                  put into generic types:

- Finance business models create financial assets
  and liabilities. Banks create money and credit.
  Non-bank financial intermediaries manage
  financial assets and risks.

- Resources business models find, finance and
  produce natural resources

- Capital goods business models build capital goods
  and create an installed base of product (hardware
  or software).

- Services business models operate installed bases of
  capital goods.

- Distribution business models distribute product to
  customers.

- Process business models process intermediate goods.

- Intellectual property business models create, sell
  and exploit intellectual property.

Discount rate   A rate per annum at which a future cashflow is
                  discounted back to the present. A nominal discount
                  rate will notionally comprise three elements: 1) a
                  real 'risk-free' rate; 2) an inflation rate; and 3) a risk
                  premium to reflect the riskiness of the assets.

The discount rate for some business cashflows may differ in different currencies – because the real risk-free rate and inflation rates may be different. Consequently an identical business in two different countries with different currencies may have different PE ratios. The different PE ratios may reflect different nominal risk-free rates rather than a valuation anomaly.

Profit

A word denoting Christmas cheer and superabundance or heartless exploitation depending upon whether one perceives one is sharing in it.

An estimate of the surplus in cash or money's worth which was created in a specific period of time arrived according to accounting conventions and approximating to smoothed cashflow.

A profit is a surplus which can be re-invested or distributed after having repaid the original capital employed. In practical terms a profit is defined as a surplus which is realised in cash – or is reasonably certain to be realisable in cash.

Profits which do not turn into cash can transpire to be 'fool's gold'.

NPV figures are very subjective and risky relative to profit numbers, which themselves are not risk free. NPVs cannot be paid in taxes or divided among shareholders because they are not cash.

Natural suspicion requires profits to be measured frequently – usually at least once a year. Measures of profits of long-term projects taken at short intervals are little better than pro tem estimates of what might or might not turn out to be profitable.

Risk-free rate

Risk-free rate is a not a literally risk-free rate but rather a manner of speaking about the least risky observable market interest rates. These are usually the interest rates on securities issued by sovereign governments.

Redemption yield or yield to maturity

The IRR of a bond.

Yield curve,
term structure

The price of credit varies with the length of time for
which it is borrowed. £100 cash receivable in one
year's time might cost 5% pa. £100 receivable in
two years' time might cost 6% pa. 5% pa is the spot
rate for one-year money and 6% pa is the 'spot rate'
for two-year money. Spot interest rates for different
years are all arithmetically linked.

In this example, the 'forward one year spot rate' for
£100 invested for one year in one year's time is 7%
$((1.06^2/1.05)-1))$.

the price of
money with
different
payment dates

In principle money paid in each different year in the
future has a different price. It is the IRR of a zero
coupon bond redeeming in that year. Each rate is
known as the 'spot rate' for the year. It is the unique
rate at which the zero coupon bond compounds.

Bonds have different redemption dates. 'Redemption
yields' are quoted for bonds. A long bond will
normally have a higher redemption yield than a short
bond. A redemption yield is a complicated average
of spot rates. So a three-year bond might have a
redemption yield of 5% (if trading at par) which
might be made up of a one year spot rate of 4%, a
two year spot rate of 5% and a three year spot rate of
6%. $\sqrt[3]{1.04 \times 1.05 \times 1.06} = 1.05$.

Strictly a yield curve is the sequence of spot rates.
Sometimes it is crudely approximated by taking the
redemption yields of bonds of different maturities.

Yield curves are commonly constructed for
government bonds and show interest rates on
3-month to 30-year maturities.

Yield curves for different types of borrowing by
different types (risk) of borrower are observable
dynamic market phenomena. http://stockcharts.
com/charts/YieldCurve.html shows the US Treasury
yield curve and provides an animation of how it has
changed over time.

Risk

Conventionally thought of as 'statistical risk' measured using 'mean variance analysis'. Mean variance analysis considers the variability of outcomes around a mean or average. This works very well for variables which are immutable across time – inanimate objects which can be 'objectively' measured – or for short periods of time. It works less well for objects which are 'meta data' – not the data itself but somebody's perception of the data – such as market prices.

The riskiness of 'processes' is less well captured by statistical analysis than the 'riskiness' of particular physical characteristics varying from an average.

Processes can be thought of as distributions of outcomes which are affected by time. In processes the average may evolve as the process moves through time and at some point the process may 'die'; that is, change completely.

The human processes which create civilisation involve freedom of choice and therefore involve responsibility for outcomes. The outcomes are not therefore 'givens' in the same way that physical outcomes are givens.

Another definition of risk for investment is the difference between price and value. The difficulty with this definition is that neither price nor value are completely objective.

Statistical definitions of risk can create a false sense of objectivity whereas consideration of value forces consideration of fundamentally difficult issues.

IRR (Internal Rate of Return)

The discount rate which happens to reduce npv to zero.

If the discount rate used is zero, the npv is the cumulative net undiscounted cashflows which will be received in the future. As the discount rate rises above zero the net present values fall. At some rate of interest, known as the internal rate of return, the net present value is zero.

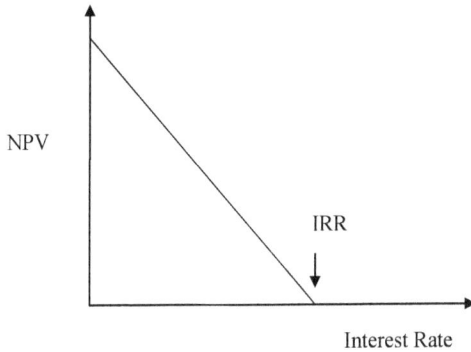

NPV

IRR

Interest Rate

Uncertainty   The elephant in the room. Variously addressed by religion, denial (oft in error but never in doubt) and banal cliches ('the market hates uncertainty').

Orthodox economics assumes away this core problem with two enormous presuppositions: 1) economic man is rational; 2) the future is rationally calculable.

Keynes wrote in *The General Theory*:

'The orthodox theory assumes that we have a knowledge of the future of a quite different kind from that we actually possess. This false rationalisation follows the line of the Benthamite calculus. The hypothesis of a calculable future leads to a wrong interpretation of the principles of behaviour which the need for action compels us to adopt, and to an underestimation of the concealed factors of utter doubt, precariousness, hope and fear.'

Classical economics treated resource allocation as a sort of linear programming problem which was solved by voluntary trading through competitive markets. The 'solution' to all the simultaneous equations is 'equilibrium'.

Market practitioners are sceptical about the notion of equilibrium. Experience suggests that price equilibrium is the exception rather than the norm, a transitory stage in a dynamic and unstable world.

Bibliography

Ernst Gombrich	*A Little History of the World*, Yale University Press, first published 1936
Martin Meredith	*The State of Africa, A History of Fifty Years of Independence*, Free Press, 2006
Carlo Cippola	*The Economic History of World Population*, Penguin Books, first published 1962
E.F. Schumacher	*Small Is Beautiful. A Study of Economics as if People Mattered*, Vintage, first published 1973
George Soros	*The Alchemy of Finance*, John Wiley & Sons, 1994
Alice Schroeder	*The Snowball: Warren Buffet and the Business of Life*, Bloomsbury Publishing, 2009
Peter L. Bernstein	*Against the Gods: The Remarkable Story of Risk*, John Wiley and Sons, New York, 1996
Ben Graham	*The Intelligent Investor*, HarperCollins, first published 1949
Andrew Smithers	*Valuing Wall Street*, John Wiley, 2009
Ralph Wanger	*A Zebra in Lion Country*, Simon & Schuster, 1997

About the Author

Ben Paton is an investment management professional.
He worked for Fidelity Investments in London for thirteen years
where he specialized in equity investment. Between 2004 and
2008 he was the lead fund manager for the Fidelity International
Smaller Companies Fund, a US mutual fund which significantly
outperformed its benchmark.

Ben has an MBA from London Business School prior to which
he worked in corporate finance and venture capital in London
and Paris. He qualified as a Chartered Accountant with Peat
Marwick after studying History & Economics at Oxford.

His interests include enjoying his family, taming his garden,
reading, skiing and listening to music

www.ingramcontent.com/pod-product-compliance
Lightning Source LLC
Chambersburg PA
CBHW071636200326
41519CB00012BA/2316